FUNNY
LADIES

FUNNY LADIES

The Best Humor from America's Funniest Women

Bill Adler

**Andrews McMeel
Publishing**

Kansas City

01 02 03 04 05 BIN 10 9 8 7 6 5 4 3 2 1

Library of Congress Cataloging-in-Publication Data

Funny ladies : the best humor from America's funniest women / [compiled by] Bill Adler.
   p. cm.
  ISBN 0-7407-0612-8 (pbk.)
   1. Women—Quotations. 2. American wit and humor. I. Adler, Bill.

PN6081.5 .F86 2001
305.6—dc21   00-064006

Book design by Lisa Martin

Contents

Contents

Contents

Acknowledgments

My deep appreciation to another funny lady, Tracy Quinn, for her dedication and hard work researching and editing this collecting.

Introduction

If you're looking for the right zinger for a lazy co-worker, a cheerful pick-me-up for a blue friend, or some words of advice or inspiration for yourself, *Funny Ladies: The Best Humor from America's Funniest Women* is a collection to cherish. You'll want to read these words of wit and wisdom from extraordinary women about success, relationships, sex, entertainment, art, children, and numerous other subjects over and over again.

Spanning more than a hundred years of funny women in America, you'll find anticipated words of wisdom—such as those from Jane Fonda on fitness, Dorothy Parker on wit, Mae West on men, and Phyllis Diller on housework—as well as surprises from some unlikely sources, such as Erica Jong on asking for advice, Ann Landers on technology, Bella Abzug on fashion, and Lillian Carter on motherhood. You'll also find funny women who have something serious to say, such as Whoopi Goldberg's opinions on race and the gender gap.

The women in *Funny Ladies* are drawn from a variety of our best wits. Some weren't even born in the United States, such as the Hungarian-born Zsa Zsa Gabor, England's Tracey Ullman, the Polish Sophie Tucker, the Italian Sophia Loren, or the Canadian Phyllis McGinley, but they immigrated to the United States and became famous. You'll also find a few women, such as Ruby Wax, who were born in the United States, lived most of their lives here, but found fame overseas. You'll find women known for playing comedic roles, such as Candice Bergen, Goldie Hawn, and Julia Louis-Dreyfus; women known specifically as stand-up comediennes, such as Rita Rudner; and stand-up comediennes who have exploded onto the entertainment scene, even finding work as the hosts or creators of their own television shows, such as Rosie O'Donnell, Carol Burnett, Roseanne, Ellen DeGeneres, and

Brett Butler. You'll even find at least one example of a funny lady who isn't a woman at all—well, at least not technically—in our own Miss Piggy.

From Jackie "Moms" Mabley and Totie Fields to Erma Bombeck and Cher, Joan Rivers and Fran Lebowitz, you'll find something on each page to make you smile, make you laugh aloud, or give you some thought.

*The greatest
thing I ever
was able to
do was give
a welfare
check back.*

—Whoopi Goldberg

Achievement and Ambition

Knowing what you can *not* do is more important than knowing what you can do. In fact, that's good taste.

—*Lucille Ball*

Attempt the impossible in order to improve your work.

—*Bette Davis*

I'm not going to limit myself just because people won't accept the fact that I can do something else.

—*Dolly Parton*

I want to do it all. I want to own the world.
— *Marsha Warfield*

I want to find myself before somebody
bigger does.
— *Carrie Fisher*

The only thing experience teaches you is what
you can't do. When you start, you think you
can do anything. And then you start to get a
little tired.
— *Elaine May*

It's not the having, it's the getting.
— *Elizabeth Taylor*

My mother always told me I wouldn't amount
to anything because I procrastinate. I said,
"Just wait."

—*Judy Tenuta*

There are people who put their dreams in a
little box and say, "Yes, I've got dreams, of
course, I've got dreams." Then they put the
box away and bring it out once in a while to
look at it, and yep, they're still there. These are
great dreams, but they never even get out of
the box. It takes an uncommon amount of
guts to put your dreams on the line, to hold
them up and say, "How good or how bad
am I?" That's where courage comes in.

—*Erma Bombeck*

My passions were all gathered together like
fingers that made a fist. Drive is considered
aggression today; I knew it then as purpose.

—*Bette Davis*

Acting and Actors

Movie actors are just ordinary mixed-up
people—with agents.

—*Jean Kerr*

I think acting is the biggest drag of all time
for a girl.

—*Jackie Collins*

You are not in business to be popular.

—*Kirstie Alley*

We have stuntpeople who won't do what
I do.

—*Molly Shannon*

Every now and then, when you're onstage,
you hear the best sound a player can hear.
It's a sound you can't get in movies or in
television. It is the sound of a wonderful,
deep silence that means you've hit them
where they live.

—*Shelley Winters*

I do not regret one professional enemy I have
made. Any actor who doesn't dare to make an
enemy should get out of the business.

—*Bette Davis*

I told her I would play a Venetian blind, dirt on the floor, anything.

—*Whoopi Goldberg*

I'm not interested in being me. I'm not that sort of actress. I like disguising myself. I get more confidence when I don't sound or look like myself. I started off impersonating people from documentaries or Ken Loach films at home after I'd watched TV at night. I used to sit in front of my mirror and pretend I was a welfare wife with my husband in prison. I just liked becoming someone who totally wasn't me.

—*Tracey Ullman*

I'm not an actress who can create a character.
I play me.

— *Mary Tyler Moore*

I'm not as klutzy as I used to be. . . . I've had
visual therapy and all kinds of things to help,
but I still wrap my purse around chair legs
when I stand up to leave. I do ridiculous
things on camera because I do them in my
life all the time.

— *Shelley Long*

Your audience gives you everything you need.
They tell you. There is no director who can
direct you like an audience.

— *Fanny Brice*

I may not be a great actress but I've become the greatest at screen orgasms. Ten seconds of heavy breathing, roll your head from side to side, simulate a slight asthma attack, and die a little.

—Candice Bergen

If there wasn't something called acting they would probably hospitalize people like me. The giddiness and the joy of life is the moving and grooving, the exploration.

—Whoopi Goldberg

Acting is a matter of giving away secrets.

—Ellen Barkin

I've made so many movies playing a hooker
that they don't pay me in the regular way
anymore. They leave it on the dresser.
                                    —*Shirley MacLaine*

She's okay if you like talent.
                    —*Ethel Merman, on her friend Mary Martin*

Acting is standing up naked and turning
around very slowly.
                                    —*Rosalind Russell*

Acting is the most minor of gifts and not a
very high-class way to earn a living. After all,
Shirley Temple could do it at the age of four.
                                    —*Katharine Hepburn*

My first experience onstage, though, was at Commodore Sloat Grammar School. I was a candidate for school office. They said, "Come up here and tell us why we should vote for you." I couldn't think of a single reason. But I got onstage and, with my knees knocking, I began to do imitations of the faculty, and they loved it! So I would go onstage every Friday and entertain. That was in the fourth grade.

— Carol Channing

Advice

What you can't get out of, get into whole-heartedly.

— Mignon McLaughlin

Keep breathing.

—*Sophie Tucker*

Cherish forever what makes you unique,
'cuz you're really a yawn if it goes!

—*Bette Midler*

Let the world know you as you are, not as you
think you should be, because sooner or later,
if you are posing, you will forget the pose, and
then where are you?

—*Fanny Brice*

You never find yourself until you face
the truth.

—*Pearl Bailey*

Never play peekaboo with a child on a long
plane trip. There's no end to the game. Finally
I grabbed him by the bib and said, "Look, it's
always gonna be me!"

— Rita Rudner

No day is so bad it can't be fixed with a nap.

— Carrie Snow

Trust your husband, adore your husband, and
get as much as you can in your own name.

— Joan Rivers

Speak up for yourself, or you'll end up a rug.

— Mae West

Let people push you around. The person who says, believes, and acts on the phrase "I ain't taking any shit from anybody" is a very busy person indeed. This person must be ever vigilant against news vendors who shortchange him, cabdrivers who take him the wrong way around, waiters who serve the other guy first, florists who are charging ten cents more per tulip than the one down the block, pharmacists who make you wait too long, and cars that cut you off at the light: they are a veritable miasma of righteous indignation and never have a minute to relax and have a good time.

—*Cynthia Heimel*

Just remember, we're all in this alone.

—*Lily Tomlin*

You have got to discover you, what you do,
and trust it.

—*Barbra Streisand*

Never accept an invitation from a stranger
unless he gives you candy.

—*Linda Festa*

There are only two important facial expres-
sions to master: completely overwhelming
unbridled joy, and nothing at all.

—*Merrill Markoe*

You can do one of two things; just shut up,
which is something I don't find easy, or learn an
awful lot very fast, which is what I tried to do.

—*Jane Fonda*

Women who insist on having the same options
as men would do well to consider the option
of being the strong, silent type.

—*Fran Lebowitz*

Nobody really cares if you're miserable, so
you might as well be happy.

—*Cynthia Nelms*

If you're going to be able to look back on
something and laugh about it, you might
as well laugh about it now.

—*Marie Osmond*

Sometimes I wonder what the difference is
between being cautious and being dead.

—*Sue Grafton*

About all you can do is be who you are. Some people will love you for you. Most will love you for what you can do for them, and some won't like you at all.

— *Rita Mae Brown*

The best way to hold a man is in your arms.

— *Mae West*

Advice is what we ask for when we already know the answer but wish we didn't.

— *Erica Jong*

If you obey all the rules, you miss all the fun.

— *Katharine Hepburn*

Resentment isn't a magnetic personal style.
— *Peggy Noonan*

He who hesitates is a damned fool.
— *Mae West*

When you are kind to someone in trouble, you hope they'll remember and be kind to someone else. And it'll become like a wildfire.
— *Whoopi Goldberg*

Never go to bed mad. Stay up and fight.
— *Phyllis Diller*

Never face facts; if you do you'll never get up in the morning.
— *Marlo Thomas*

Never go to a doctor whose office plants
have died.

—*Erma Bombeck*

Age and Aging

I believe in loyalty. When a woman reaches
a certain age she likes, she should stick
with it.

—*Eva Gabor*

We are always the same age inside.

—*Gertrude Stein*

I am very attractive and get cuter the older I get. I'm even getting—well, not statuesque, but I'm growing. I'm expanding. That's the best way to put it.

— *Whoopi Goldberg*

I've changed my attitudes about what it means to age. Sometimes people decide it's their lot in life to be old, but people like Grandma bring color and excellence to their lives. That's what I've tried to do, too. I'm looking forward to the next stage.

— *Cloris Leachman*

Now that I'm over sixty, I'm veering toward respectability.

— *Shelley Winters*

Women are not forgiven for aging. Robert
Redford's lines of distinction are my old age
wrinkles.

—*Jane Fonda*

Age is something that doesn't matter, unless
you are a cheese.

—*Billie Burke*

Someone asked someone who was about my
age, "How are you?" The answer was, "Fine.
If you don't ask details."

—*Katharine Hepburn*

As you get older, the pickings get slimmer, but
the people don't.

—*Carrie Fisher*

I'm like old wine. They don't bring me out very often, but I'm well preserved.

—Rose Kennedy

I believe the true function of age is memory.
I'm recording as fast as I can.

—Rita Mae Brown

We look into mirrors, but we only see the
effects of our times on us—not our effects
on others.

—Pearl Bailey

My forties are the best time I have ever gone
through.

—Elizabeth Taylor

Old age is when the liver spots show through
your gloves.

—Phyllis Diller

There *is* a fountain of youth: It is your mind, your talents, the creativity you bring to your life and the lives of the people you love. When you learn to tap this source, you will truly have defeated age.

— *Sophia Loren*

I don't feel the effect of years because age, to me, is learning, and the quest for understanding is more important than how many wrinkles I have or how high I can kick when I dance.

— *Phylicia Rashad*

The secret to staying young is to live honestly, eat slowly, and lie about your age.

— *Lucille Ball*

I see myself at about twelve. And it's really interesting. My grandmother—what is she, eighty-eight? One time, a few years ago, I was looking at her and remembering her when she was younger, and I was real little. I remember her wearing cocktail dresses and earrings and gloves, looking real glamorous, even though she wasn't all that young even then. I asked her, "How old do you feel?" She said, "I haven't felt different since I was seventeen. Even when I see this old, wrinkled woman in the mirror, I still think of myself as being about seventeen. It doesn't ever really change." It frightens me that one day it's gonna be, like, menopause! That I'm going to wake up and start being crabby and not want to go to Disneyland or do other childlike things that

I still do now. And yet I think I have a kind
of maturity that comes only with age.

—*Cher*

From birth to age eighteen, a girl needs
good parents. From eighteen to thirty-five,
she needs good looks. From thirty-five to
fifty-five, she needs a good personality.
From fifty-five on, she needs good cash.

—*Sophie Tucker*

I was forced to live far beyond my years
when I was just a child; now I have reversed
the order and I intend to remain young
indefinitely.

—*Mary Pickford*

I felt that when I turned fifty, life was starting
for me. . . . You make a choice. You wake up
in the morning, and you make a choice. You
either pack it in and decide that life is awful,
or you take your moments and invest in them,
honor them, honor yourself, and live them to
the fullest.

— *Goldie Hawn*

I was born in 1962. True. And the room
next to me was 1963.

— *Joan Rivers*

A woman who will tell her age will tell
anything.

— *Rita Mae Brown*

I feel that you reach a ccrtain age and then things start to jell. My sense of self is stronger. I'm getting bolder in my old age. After I hit forty, you couldn't mess around with me so much anymore.

—*Julie Kavner*

Before we came along, a woman who reached forty or so became invisible . . . so they slid into being boring matrons or dotty eccentrics. Only the young wore interesting clothes. But we're not like that anymore. . . . We're still running around trying to have adventures. We're constantly reinventing ourselves. And we could use a few outfits.

—*Cynthia Heimel*

My grandmother started walking five miles
a day when she was sixty. She's ninety-seven
now, and we don't know where the hell she is.
— *Ellen DeGeneres*

The really frightening thing about middle age
is the knowledge that you'll grow out of it.
— *Doris Day*

Old age ain't no place for sissies.
— *Bette Davis*

A woman past forty should make up her mind
to be young, not her face.
— *Billie Burke*

Appearance and Beauty

I'm tired of all this nonsense of beauty being only skin deep. That's enough. What do you want, an adorable pancreas?

—*Jean Kerr*

I look just like the girl next door . . . if you happen to live next door to an amusement park.

—*Dolly Parton*

It's a good thing beauty is only skin deep, or I'd be rotten to the core.

—*Phyllis Diller*

When I'm an old lady, I'm going to get my nails done twice a week. As good as red nails look, when they start to chip, it's like the cheap-prostitute look.

—*Julia Louis-Dreyfus*

My husband said he wanted to have a relationship with a redhead, so I dyed my hair.

—*Jane Fonda*

Beauty comes in all sizes—not just size 5.

—*Roseanne*

When you're not thin and blond, you come up with a personality real quick.

—*Kathy Najimy*

This business manipulates and screws up women's—and men's—views of what we're all supposed to look like. . . . My gender-bender style is apparently a bore.

—*Ellen DeGeneres, on appearing on a "worst dressed" list*

I blame those damn *Friends* girls. Who can be that skinny? Well, I wanted to be, so I got liposuction. You see, I am a size 4—which is, apparently, by Hollywood standards, a real cow! Most actresses on television are a 2 or a 0 or maybe a child's size 6X.

—*Kathy Griffin*

Ask any girl what she'd rather be than beautiful, and she'll say more beautiful.

—*Martha Raye*

FUNNY LADIES

I think onstage nudity is disgusting, shameful,
and damaging to all things American. But if
I were twenty-two with a great body, it would
be artistic, tasteful, patriotic, and a progressive
religious experience.

—Shelley Winters

You never see a man walking down the street
with a woman who has a little potbelly and a
bald spot.

—Elayne Boosler

I think your whole life shows in your face and
you should be proud of that.

—Lauren Bacall

When I go to the beauty parlor, I always use the emergency entrance. Sometimes I go just for an estimate.

—Phyllis Diller

It's okay to be fat. So you're fat. Just be fat and shut up about it.

—Roseanne

I'm not offended by all the dumb blonde jokes because I know I'm not dumb . . . and I also know I'm not blonde.

—Dolly Parton

I don't do T and A very well because I haven't got much of either.

—Téa Leoni

If truth is
beauty, how
come no one
has their
hair done in
a library?

— Lily Tomlin

Guys are lucky because they get to grow
mustaches. I wish I could. It's like having
a pet for your face.

—*Anita Wise*

Being a sex symbol has to do with an attitude,
not looks. Most men think it's looks, most
women know otherwise.

—*Kathleen Turner*

People are constantly telling me how much
alike you and I are.

—*Totie Fields, to Jayne Mansfield*

Mirrors lie. You are much better looking than
that in 3-D.

—*Merrill Markoe*

I think of my body as a side effect of my mind.
Like a thought I had once that manifested
itself—Oops! Oh no! Manifested. Look at this.
Now we have to buy clothes and everything.

—*Carrie Fisher*

The psychic scars caused by believing that
you are ugly leave a permanent mark on
your personality.

—*Joan Rivers*

People get real comfortable with their features.
Nobody gets comfortable with their hair.
Hair trauma. It's the universal thing.

—*Jamie Lee Curtis*

The most common error made in matters
of appearance is the belief that one should
disdain the superficial and let the true beauty
of one's soul shine through. If there are places
on your body where this is a possibility, you
are not attractive—you are leaking.

— *Fran Lebowitz*

It's really a joke that my whole life people
thought I was unattractive until now—when
I'm getting too old to really be attractive.

— *Cher*

I don't want to say I'm envious of any other
woman's body. It's a bad myth to perpetuate.
Women have enough trouble liking themselves.

— *Teri Garr*

I have heard men say that they don't mind the idea of breast implants in a woman because, after all, big breasts are big breasts. On the other hand, I have never met a woman who would rather be with a man in a toupee than a bald man.

—Merrill Markoe

I can't postpone my life until I lose weight. I have to live right now.

—Delta Burke

I don't have to be well informed. I'm well endowed. I'm a star.

—Bette Midler

A feller told me last night I was a breath of fresh air. Well, he didn't exactly put it that way. He said I looked like the end of a long, hard winter.

—*Minnie Pearl*

I had been fed, in my youth, a lot of old wives' tales about the way men would instantly forsake a beautiful woman to flock around a brilliant one. It is but fair to say that, after getting out in the world, I had never seen this happen.

—*Dorothy Parker*

A smile is the cheapest way to improve your looks, even if your teeth are crooked.

—*Ann Landers*

FUNNY LADIES

If I hadn't had them, I would have had
some made.

—Dolly Parton, *on her breasts*

I've got a sitting with Caravaggio in the
morning, and if that man doesn't see cellulite,
I'm history.

—Joy Behar, *to a waiter*

I do have this quality that is very childlike.
But how long can it last? How long can you
be cute?

—Goldie Hawn

It is better to be looked over than overlooked.

—Mae West

The reason I come off being sexy and attractive—I still can't bring myself to say "pretty"—is because I have had myself rebuilt. I had the hair under my arms taken care of. And I had an operation to firm up my breasts. And I spend about a thousand dollars a week to have my toenails, fingernails, eyebrows, and hair put in top shape. I'm the female equivalent of a counterfeit twenty-dollar bill. Half of what you see is a pretty good reproduction, and the rest is a fraud.

—Cher

I walk out of a rest room with my dress stuck in the top of my panty hose, and I have the audacity to think everyone is noticing me because I'm such a beauty.

—Mary Ellen Hooper

Plain women know more about men than beautiful ones do.

—Katharine Hepburn

I have everything I had twenty years ago, only it's all a little bit lower.

—Gypsy Rose Lee

People see you as an object, not as a person, and they project a set of expectations onto you. People who don't have it think beauty is a blessing, but actually it sets you apart.

—Candice Bergen

I don't have false teeth. Do you think I'd buy teeth like these?

—Carol Burnett

Lots of women buy just as many wigs and makeup things as I do. . . . They just don't wear them all at the same time.

— Dolly Parton

Art and Artists, Music and Musicians

I think most of the people involved in any art always secretly wonder whether they are really there because they're good—or because they're lucky.

— Katharine Hepburn

Art is the signature of civilizations.

— Beverly Sills

Rap is poetry set to music. But to me it's like a jackhammer.

—*Bette Midler*

I don't want life to imitate art. I want life to be art.

—*Carrie Fisher*

An unalterable and unquestioned law of the musical world required that the German text of French operas sung by Swedish artists should be translated into Italian for the clearer understanding of English-speaking audiences.

—*Edith Wharton*

Blues is rap, just singing it.

—*Queen Latifah (Dana Owens)*

If I hadn't started painting, I would have raised chickens.

—Grandma Moses

Classical music is music written by famous dead foreigners.

—Arlene Heath

I rap lite on "I'm Beautiful." I have an excellent sense of time. I was thinking of taking up the bass or drums because I like rhythm. The problem is, I have nothing to say. What am I going to rap about? My hairdresser? My nails? Actually, that could be fun.

—Bette Midler

I'm an artist; art has no color and no sex.

—Whoopi Goldberg

When I was a little kid I thought I would grow up to be black and sing jazz in nightclubs.
—*Molly Ringwald*

I thought black people had it bad, but I never knew how bad you white people had it until I started listening to country music.
—*Emmy Gay*

Birth Control and Abortion

It serves me right for putting all my eggs in one bastard.
—*Dorothy Parker, on her abortion*

I rely on my personality for birth control.
— Liz Winston

If one is willing to have children, rhythm is probably the best method of birth control.
— Elizabeth Hawes

Soon a cop will be at the door saying,
"So, I hear you had a miscarriage. Prove it."
— Reno (Karen Renaud) on the
Supreme Court abortion ruling

If men could get pregnant, abortion would be a sacrament.
— Florynce Kennedy

When my mom found my diaphragm, I told
her it was a bathing cap for my cat.

— *Liz Winston*

Books and Reading

Fitting people with books is about as difficult
as fitting them with shoes.

— *Sylvia Beach*

A list of our authors who have made themselves most beloved and, therefore, most
comfortable financially, shows that it is our
national joy to mistake for the first-rate, the
fecund rate.

— *Dorothy Parker*

The biggest critics of my books are people
who never read them.

—*Jackie Collins*

A bit of trash now and then is good for the
severest reader. It provides the necessary
roughage in the literary diet.

—*Phyllis McGinley*

I've always thought that if my death was
imminent, I would read. When I can't focus
on a book, I tend to keep reading the same
page. My guess is, I would've read, like,
the first page of *Nicholas Nickleby* over and
over again.

—*Paula Poundstone*

Self-help books are making life downright
unsafe. Women desperate to catch a man
practice all the ploys recommended by these
authors. Bump into him, trip over him, knock
him down, spill something on him, scald him,
but meet him.

—*Florence King*

I read a book twice as fast as anybody else.
First, I read the beginning, and then I read
the ending, and then I start in the middle
and read toward whatever end I like best.

—*Gracie Allen*

Having been unpopular in high school is not
just cause for book publications.

—*Fran Lebowitz*

I always read the last page of a book first so that if I die before I finish I'll know how it turned out.

— Nora Ephron

I'll be eighty this month. Age, if nothing else, entitles me to set the record straight before I dissolve. I've given my memoirs far more thought than any of my marriages. You can't divorce a book.

— Gloria Swanson

The buying of a self-help book is the most desperate of all human acts. It means you've lost your mind completely: You've entrusted your mental health to a self-aggrandizing twit with a psychology degree and a yen for a yacht.

— Cynthia Heimel

Critics: People who make monuments out of books. Biographers: People who make books out of monuments. Poets: People who raze monuments. Publishers: People who sell rubble. Readers: People who buy it.

—*Cynthia Ozick*

Challenges

Into every life a little rain must fall, but I think someone's mistaken me for Noah.

—*Allison Raul*

If you really want something, you can figure out how to make it happen.

—*Cher*

I have become my own version of an optimist.
If I can't make it through one door, I'll go
through another door—or I'll make a door.
Something terrific will come no matter how
dark the present.

—Joan Rivers

Every time I think I've touched bottom as far
as boredom is concerned, new vistas of ennui
open up.

—Margaret Halsey

Opportunity knocked. My doorman threw
him out.

—Adrienne Gusoff

I eat when I'm depressed, I buy shoes when I'm jealous, I break the telephone when I'm angry, I mangle my fingernails when I'm lonely, I throw things all over the house when I'm hurt, and I waste money on makeup when I'm frustrated. Men just don't know how to cope.

—*Cathy Guisewite*

The way I see it, if you want the rainbow, you gotta put up with the rain.

—*Dolly Parton*

When something [an affliction] happens to you, you either let it defeat you, or you defeat it.

—*Rosalind Russell*

I have always grown from my problems and challenges, from the things that don't work out, that's when I've really learned.

—*Carol Burnett*

Trouble is a part of your life, and if you don't share it, you don't give the person who loves you a chance to love you enough.

—*Dinah Shore*

If you can keep your head when all about are losing theirs, it's just possible you haven't grasped the situation.

—*Jean Kerr*

Things are going to get a lot worse before they get worse.

—*Lily Tomlin*

I'm not afraid of too many things, and
I got that invincible kind of attitude from
[my father].

—*Queen Latifah (Dana Owens)*

You can't be brave if you've only had
wonderful things happen to you.

—*Mary Tyler Moore*

Childhood and Growing Up

Remember that as a teenager you are in the
last stage of your life when you will be happy
to hear the phone is for you.

—*Fran Lebowitz*

When I was a kid I had two friends, and they were imaginary, and they would only play with each other.

—Rita Rudner

I was never a child. I was always a menopausal woman in a child's body.

—Tracey Ullman

Revivals used to come to town. They would ask who wanted to be saved and I'd march right to the front. It was then that I knew I was destined for a career in show business, or at least alcoholism.

—Brett Butler

I didn't belong as a kid, and that always bothered me. If only I'd known that one day my differentness would be an asset, then my early life would have been much easier.

— *Bette Midler*

It was no great tragedy being Judy Garland's daughter. I had tremendously interesting childhood years—except they had little to do with being a child.

— *Liza Minnelli*

I was always an observer. I would observe rather than partake, and I don't think that is too hip a thing to do when you're fifteen.

— *Ruby Wax*

The hardest part about being a kid is knowing
you have got your whole life ahead of you.
                              —*Jane Wagner*

The young are generally full of revolt, and are
often pretty revolting about it.
                              —*Mignon McLaughlin*

Maturity: A stoic response to endless reality.
                              —*Carrie Fisher*

When my mom got really mad, she would say,
"Your butt is my meat." Not a particularly
attractive phrase. And I always wondered,
Now, what wine goes with that?
                              —*Paula Poundstone*

We didn't exactly starve, but we were pretty poor when I was growing up. I remember thinking, Oh gosh, if I could just make thirty dollars a month to help with the rent, that would be fabulous. So perhaps I envied performers when I heard that Bing Crosby made twenty dollars a minute.

— *Carol Burnett*

From the moment I was six I felt sexy. And let me tell you it was hell, sheer hell, waiting to do something about it.

— *Bette Davis*

Growing up is the best revenge.

— *Judith Martin, Miss Manners*

When I was a kid I would get upset when
people laughed at me when I didn't mean
to be funny. I would always hear, "We're not
laughing at you. We're laughing with you."
But I would say, "*I'm* not laughing."

—*Julie Kavner*

I was so surprised at being born that I didn't
speak for a year and a half.

—*Gracie Allen*

My mom was a ventriloquist and she always
was throwing her voice. For ten years I thought
the dog was telling me to kill my father.

—*Wendy Liebman*

My parents . . . had decided early on that all of the problems in my family had somehow to do with me. All roads led to Roseyville, a messy, chaotic town where, as parents, they were required to visit but could never get out of quick enough or find a decent parking place.

—*Roseanne*

By the time I'd grown up, I naturally supposed that I'd grown up.

—*Eve Babitz*

I wasn't used to children and they were getting on my nerves. Worse, it appeared that I was a child, too. I hadn't known that before; I thought I was just short.

—*Florence King, on her first day of kindergarten*

I think of birth as the search for a larger
apartment.

—*Rita Mae Brown*

Children

Children do not really need money.
After all, they don't have to pay rent or
send Mailgrams.

—*Fran Lebowitz*

Children are a house's enemy. They don't
mean to be—they just can't help it. It's their
enthusiasm, their energy, their naturally
destructive tendencies.

—*Delia Ephron*

They have big egos, a lot of them—if they are not crushed. You can think you are the center of the universe.

—*Ruby Wax, on being an only child*

All parents believe their children can do the impossible. They thought it the minute we were born, and no matter how hard we've tried to prove them wrong, they all think it about us now. And the really annoying thing is, they're probably right.

—*Cathy Guisewite*

Experts say you should never hit your children in anger. When is a good time? When you're feeling festive?

—*Roseanne*

Every minute
with a child
takes seven
minutes off
your life.

—Barbara Kingsolver

With any child entering adolescence, one hunts for signs of health, is desperate for the smallest indication that the child's problems will never be important enough for a television movie.

— *Nora Ephron*

A child develops individuality long before he develops taste. I have seen my kid straggle into the kitchen in the morning with outfits that need only one accessory: an empty gin bottle.

— *Erma Bombeck*

Ask your child what he wants for dinner only if he's buying.

— *Fran Lebowitz*

Kids love to see me coming. Compared to most of the three-year-olds they know, I am a major slacker. My idea of an educational field trip is to pop them in the car and drive through the car wash screaming.

— *Kate Clinton*

The best way to keep children at home is to make the home atmosphere pleasant—and let the air out of their tires.

— *Dorothy Parker*

Children are different—mentally, physically, spiritually, quantitatively, qualitatively; and furthermore, they're all a bit nuts.

— *Jean Kerr*

Be nice to your children, for they will choose
your rest home.

—*Phyllis Diller*

Children always take the line of most
persistence.

—*Marcelene Cox*

You have a wonderful child. Then, when he's
thirteen, gremlins carry him away and leave
in his place a stranger who gives you not a
moment's peace.

—*Jill Eikenberry*

I will never understand children. I never pretended to. I meet mothers all the time who make resolutions to themselves. "I'm going to . . . go out of my way to show them I am interested in them and what they do. I am going to understand my children." These women end up making rag rugs, using blunt scissors.

— *Erma Bombeck*

Conversation and Communication

Verbal ability is a highly overrated thing in a guy, and it's our pathetic need for it that gets us into so much trouble.

— *Nora Ephron*

I personally think we developed language
because of our deep need to complain.
— Lily Tomlin

There are very few people who don't become
more interesting when they stop talking.
— Mary Lowry

The opposite of talking isn't listening.
The opposite of talking is waiting.
— Fran Lebowitz

Words, once they are printed, have a life of
their own.
— Carol Burnett

Sticks and stones are hard on bones.
Aimed with angry art,
Words can sting like anything.
But silence breaks the heart.

—*Phyllis McGinley*

The only men I really communicate with are
the ones I'll never speak to again.

—*Cathy Guisewite*

Forget grammar and think potatoes.

—*Gertrude Stein*

The conversational overachiever is someone
whose grasp exceeds his reach. This is possible
but not attractive.

—*Fran Lebowitz*

If you can't be direct, why be?

—*Lily Tomlin*

The next best thing to being clever is being able to quote someone who is.

—*Mary Pettibone Poole*

Of course we women gossip on occasion. But our appetite for it is not as avid as a man's. It is in the boys' gyms, the college fraternity houses, the club locker rooms, the paneled offices of business that gossip reaches its luxuriant flower.

—*Phyllis McGinley*

Can we talk?

—*Joan Rivers*

73

No one really listens to anyone else, and if you
try it for a while you'll see why.

—*Mignon McLaughlin*

The telephone is a good way to talk to people
without having to offer them a drink.

—*Fran Lebowitz*

Cynicism is an unpleasant way of saying
the truth.

—*Lillian Hellman*

Actions lie louder than words.

—*Carolyn Wells*

It's far more impressive when others discover your good qualities without your help.
—*Judith Martin, Miss Manners*

I never know how much of what I say is true. If I did, I'd bore myself to death.
—*Bette Midler*

A person who talks fast often says things she hasn't thought of yet.
—*Caron Warner Lieber*

Is there grammar in a title? There is grammar in a title. Thank you.
—*Gertrude Stein*

Creativity and Imagination

I can always be distracted by love, but eventually I get horny for my creativity.

—*Gilda Radner*

Delusions of grandeur make me feel a lot better about myself.

—*Jane Wagner*

I'm not going to throw my imagination away. I refuse to lie down to expectation. If I can just hold out till I'm thirty, I'll be incredible.

—*Wendy Wasserstein*

When I was in second grade, we had to color the fruits their right colors, but I colored them all yellow. The teacher said, "Don't you know that an apple is red and an orange is orange?" I said, "Yes, but I like yellow."

— Goldie Hawn

When in doubt, make a fool of yourself. There is a microscopically thin line between being brilliantly creative and acting like the most gigantic idiot on earth. So what the hell, leap.

— Cynthia Heimel

Creativity comes from trust. Trust your instincts. And never hope more than you work.

— Rita Mae Brown

Death

Big deal! I'm used to dust.
>   —*Erma Bombeck's requested epitaph*

They say you shouldn't say nothin' about the dead unless it's good. He's dead. Good!
>   —*Jackie "Moms" Mabley*

I tried to commit suicide by sticking my head in the oven, but there was a cake in it.
>   —*Lesley Boone*

In New York City, one suicide in ten is attributed to a lack of storage space.
>   —*Judith Stone*

It is so hard for us little human beings to
accept this deal that we get. It's really crazy,
isn't it? We get to live, then we have to die.
What we put into every moment is all we
have. . . . What spirit human beings have! It *is*
a pretty cheesy deal—all the pleasures of life,
and then death.

—*Gilda Radner*

Millions long for immortality who don't know
what to do on a rainy afternoon.

—*Susan Ertz*

I don't want to die. I think death is a greatly
overrated experience.

—*Rita Mae Brown*

There will be sex after death; we just won't be
able to feel it.

— Lily Tomlin

The dying process begins the minute you are
born, but it accelerates during dinner parties.

— Carol Matthau

I think we should look forward to death more
than we do. Of course everybody hates to go
to bed or miss anything, but dying is really the
only chance we'll get to rest.

— Florynce Kennedy

Domestic Life

Most turkeys taste better the day after; my
mother's tasted better the day before.

—Rita Rudner

If your house is really a mess and a stranger
comes to the door, greet him with, "Who
could have done this? We have no enemies."

—Phyllis Diller

What my mother believed about cooking
is that if you worked hard and prospered,
someone else would do it for you.

—Nora Ephron

It's nothing short of a miracle that for years
women have worked together side by side in
the kitchens of America. I would have been
willing to bet in an atmosphere of blunt
instruments and sharp cutlery, not one of
them would have been left alive.

— *Erma Bombeck*

My idea of superwoman is someone who
scrubs her own floors.

— *Bette Midler*

I will clean house when Sears comes out with
a riding vacuum cleaner.

— *Roseanne*

I have too many fantasies to be a housewife.
I guess I am a fantasy.

—*Marilyn Monroe*

I'm an excellent housekeeper. Every time
I get a divorce, I keep the house.

—*Zsa Zsa Gabor*

Sexually active coat hangers are at their
peak when they are in a small closet. We once
lived in an apartment with a closet so small
it couldn't support a rod . . . just two nails.
Within a week (the shortest gestation in the
history of coat hangers) we had thirty-seven
of those little suckers.

—*Erma Bombeck*

My mother is such a lousy cook that Thanksgiving at her house is a time of sorrow.

—*Rita Rudner*

Housework can't kill you, but why take
a chance?

—*Phyllis Diller*

So I live in this apartment that's disgusting—
it's really dirty. And the kitchen floor is, like,
sticky. And I had to do something about it.
So finally I went out and bought some,
uh, slippers.

—*Sarah Silverman*

A man in the house is worth two on the street.

—*Mae West*

The pleasure of the mulch pile is incomprehensible. I wouldn't care if they just hauled the mulch to the landfill somewhere. Obviously, grass clippings are biodegradable, but when they're bunched together at the landfill, they become badly influenced by other garbage.

—*Paula Poundstone*

Whenever I get married I start buying *Gourmet* magazine.

—*Nora Ephron*

If it weren't for women, men would still be wearing last week's socks.

—*Cynthia Nelms*

I buried a lot of my ironing in the backyard.
>—*Phyllis Diller*

I hate housework! You make the beds, you do
the dishes—and six months later you have to
start all over again.
>—*Joan Rivers*

I refuse to believe that trading recipes is silly.
Tuna-fish casserole is at least as real as
corporate stock.
>—*Barbara Grizzuti Harrison*

Housekeeping ain't no joke.
>—*Louisa May Alcott*

I was thirty-
two when
I started
cooking; up
until then,
I just ate.

—Julia Child

I don't like the terms *housewife* and *homemaker*.
I prefer to be called Domestic Goddess . . . it's
more descriptive.

—*Roseanne*

Men cook more, and we all know why. It is
the only interesting household task. Getting
down and scrubbing the floor is done by
women, or by the women they've hired.

—*Nora Ephron*

Cleaning your house while your kids are still
growing is like shoveling the walk before it
stops snowing.

—*Phyllis Diller*

Entertainment: Film, Television, and Stage

No one ever went broke in Hollywood underestimating the intelligence of the public.
—*Elsa Maxwell*

I like to do the unexpected. I never let it be the same for me. Even if it's a song I've sung before, or a role I've been doing for six months, each time is the first time. That would make some people I know very nervous. Their security depends on knowing exactly where they are and exactly what they're doing. I have to go someplace else, I have to find a new life.
—*Bernadette Peters*

Broadway has been very good to me. But I've been very good to Broadway, too.

—*Ethel Merman*

When you've got the personality, you don't need the nudity.

—*Mae West*

I didn't quite feel right doing the TV series [*Oh Madeline*], so when *Born Yesterday* came up, I thought, I started on the stage, I should go back there. On the one hand, I can criticize myself for not staying on one road. On the other hand, not everyone had the opportunity to try all these things—and you really don't know what feels best until you try it.

—*Madeline Kahn*

Television has proved that people will look at anything rather than each other.

—Ann Landers

Moral passion without entertainment is propaganda, and entertainment without moral passion is television.

—Rita Mae Brown

I wouldn't do nudity in films. To act with my clothes on is a performance. To act with my clothes off is a documentary.

—Julia Roberts

Hollywood is like Picasso's bathroom.

—Candice Bergen

If a man is pictured chopping off a woman's breast, it only gets an R rating; but if, God forbid, a man is pictured kissing a woman's breast, it gets an X rating. Why is violence more acceptable than tenderness?

—*Sally Struthers*

It is just four weeks into the new television season, and already you can't tell the pregnancies, the false alarms, and the in vitro fertilizations without a scorecard.

—*Caryn James*

You can't find any true closeness in Hollywood because everybody does the fake closeness so well.

—*Carrie Fisher*

Everyone wants to be a star in [America], don't they? You know that they're getting actors and actresses to do those shows, or they just say, "We'll pay you to sit and scream at your girlfriend." And I love when you find the one person who's been on, like, five different shows, so they can't be used anymore. I was woman with constant rash on *Geraldo,* and now I'm woman whose boyfriend beats me on *Jerry Springer.*

—Tracey Ullman, on talk shows

There are days when any electrical appliance in the house, including the vacuum cleaner, offers more entertainment than the TV set.

—Harriet Van Horne

Nonsense, all of it. Sunnybrook Farm is now a parking lot; the petticoats are in the garbage can, where they belong in the modern world; and I *detest* censorship.

—Shirley Temple Black

It struck me that the movies had spent more than half a century saying, "They lived happily ever after" and the following quarter century warning that they'll be lucky to make it through the weekend. Possibly now we are entering a third era, in which the movies will be sounding a note of cautious optimism: You know, it just might work.

—Nora Ephron

Hollywood's a place where they'll pay you a thousand dollars for a kiss, and fifty cents for your soul.

—Marilyn Monroe

There are two kinds of directors in the theater: Those who think they are God and those who are certain of it.

—Rhetta Hughes

There are only three ages for women in Hollywood—Babe, District Attorney, and Driving Miss Daisy.

—Goldie Hawn

Hollywood—an emotional Detroit.

—Lillian Gish

If I could tell you what it meant, there would be no point in dancing it.

—Isadora Duncan

I was born at the age of twelve on a Metro-Goldwyn-Mayer lot.

—Judy Garland

In Hollywood now when people die they don't say, "Did he leave a will?" but "Did he leave a diary?"

—Liza Minnelli

When the grandmothers of today hear the word *Chippendales,* they don't necessarily think of chairs.

—Jean Kerr

Right now I think censorship is necessary; the things they're doing and saying in films right now just shouldn't be allowed. There's no dignity anymore, and I think that's very important.

— *Mae West*

It would have been more logical if silent pictures had grown out of the talkies instead of the other way around.

— *Mary Pickford*

Faith and Religion

Crucifixes are sexy because there's a naked man on them.

— *Madonna*

Why do people in churches seem like cheerful, brainless tourists on a packaged tour of the Absolute?

—*Annie Dillard*

All religions are the same. Religion is basically guilt with different holidays.

—*Cathy Ladman*

Most sermons sound to me like commercials— but I can't make out whether God is the Sponsor or the Product.

—*Mignon McLaughlin*

God is love, but get it in writing.

—*Gypsy Rose Lee*

Q: Most people know you as a comedian, but recently you've gotten religious. Tell us about your efforts to promote Judyism.

A: People need something to believe in, so why not me? Judyism. In my religion, only I get to whine.

Q: Does this ever conflict with your Catholic schoolgirl upbringing?

A: Everything conflicts with my Catholic school upbringing.

—*Judy Tenuta*

What if there had been room at the inn?
—*Linda Festa, speculating on
the beginning of Christianity*

Why is it that when we talk to God we're said to be praying, but when God talks to us we're schizophrenic?

— Lily Tomlin

In the beginning there was nothing. God said, "Let there be light!" And there was light. There was still nothing, but you could see it a whole lot better.

— Ellen DeGeneres

Everyone thinks I'm Jewish. I'm not. Last year I got a call: "Happy Hanukkah." I said, "Ma, I'm not Jewish."

— Joy Behar

The worst moment for an atheist is when he feels grateful and has no one to thank.

—*Wendy Ward*

We often pray to be better, when in truth we only want to feel better.

—*Mignon McLaughlin*

Fame

In the final analysis, it's true that fame is unimportant. No matter how great a man is, the size of his funeral usually depends on the weather.

—*Rosemary Clooney*

I suck my thumb a lot.
> —*Julie Andrews, answering a question
> about how it feels to be famous*

I'd probably be famous now if I wasn't such
a good waitress.
> —*Jane Siberry*

Know the difference between success and
fame. Success is Mother Teresa. Fame is
Madonna.
> —*Erma Bombeck*

But my biggest problem all my life was men.
I never met one yet who could compete with
the image the public made out of Bette Davis.
> —*Bette Davis*

One of the first people we hired [at my new show] was a young receptionist. She answers the phone like she's doing time. A friend who called me at the office said that when he asked, "Is Paula there?" the helpful reply was, "Paula who?" Clinton has it a little easier here. If someone calls and asks, "Is the president in?" the receptionist doesn't really need to know the first name.

—*Paula Poundstone*

In Hollywood, an equitable divorce means each party getting 50 percent of publicity.

—*Lauren Bacall*

Everybody in my house knows me.

—*Paula Poundstone, on being recognized*

103

Celebrity was a long time in coming; it will
go away. Everything goes away.
— *Carol Burnett*

I've been invited into [people's] homes for
so many years, they feel like they know me.
. . . They greet me like an old friend by saying, "Hey, Betty, how are you? My back is
killing me."
— *Betty White*

Fame means being afraid some guy is going
to come up to me on the street and say, "Hey,
didn't we have sex at Woodstock?" and sell the
story to some slime-bucket magazine.
— *Whoopi Goldberg*

The Friars Club [is] like a gay bar without the cute guys.

—*Joy Behar*

I don't approve of people talking about their private lives.

—*Diane Keaton*

You know how you can get your picture on a fake magazine cover? Every time I saw [the magazine] on a newsstand, I thought they'd put out a fake *Newsweek* that week.

—*Rosie O'Donnell*

A career is born in public—talent in privacy.

—*Marilyn Monroe*

I'm a big star. I do my own shopping.

—Tracey Ullman

I stopped believing in Santa Claus at an early age. Mother took me to see him in a department store and he asked me for my autograph.
　　　　　　　　　　　　—*Shirley Temple Black*

I'm never going to be famous. I don't do anything, not one single thing. I used to bite my nails, but I don't even do that anymore.
　　　　　　　　　　　　—*Dorothy Parker*

Celebrities used to be found in clusters, like oysters—and with much the same defensive mechanisms.
　　　　　　　　　　　　—*Barbara Walters*

Bad press put me where I am. If they didn't write about me at all, I wouldn't be famous.
　　　　　　　　　　　　—*Delta Burke*

I have been attacked by Rush Limbaugh on the air, an experience somewhat akin to being gummed by a newt.

—*Molly Ivins*

Families and Parents

[My grandmother was] a very tough cookie. She buried three husbands. Two of them were just napping.

—*Rita Rudner*

My sister and I never engaged in sibling rivalry. Our parents weren't that crazy about either one of us.

—*Erma Bombeck*

I don't visit my parents often because Delta AirLines won't wait in the yard while I run in.
— *Margaret Smith*

We never talked, my family. We communicated by putting Ann Landers articles on the refrigerator.
— *Judy Gold*

My mother could make anybody feel guilty— she used to get letters of apology from people she didn't even know.
— *Joan Rivers*

My mom had the breakdown for the family, and I went into therapy for all of us.
— *Carrie Fisher*

I remember the first time we bought Uncle Nabob a store-boughten suit. It had two pairs of pants! That was nice for the winter, but wearin' both pairs got awfully hot come summer.

— *Minnie Pearl*

You think you have a handle on God, the Universe, and the Great White Light until you go home for Thanksgiving. In an hour, you realize how far you've got to go and who is the real turkey.

— *Shirley MacLaine*

She's descended from a long line her mother listened to.

— *Gypsy Rose Lee*

The thing to remember about fathers is, they're men. A girl has to keep it in mind: They are dragon seekers, bent on improbable rescues. Scratch any father, you find someone chock-full of qualms and romantic terrors, believing change is a threat—like your first shoes with heels on, like your first bicycle it took such months to get.

— *Phyllis McGinley*

I come from a family where gravy is considered a beverage.

— *Erma Bombeck*

Adopted kids are such a pain—you have to teach them how to look like you.

— *Gilda Radner*

111

And there's my Uncle Nabob. He's no failure.
He just started at the bottom and he liked it
there. One time, Nabob went into a blacksmith shop and he picked up a red-hot horseshoe and dropped it right off. "Burned ya,
didn't it?" the blacksmith said. And Nabob
said, "Why, no, it just don't take me long to
look at a horseshoe!"

—*Minnie Pearl*

I told my mother-in-law that my house was
her house, and she said, "Get the hell off my
property."

—*Joan Rivers*

Most of us became parents long before we
stopped being children.

—*Mignon McLaughlin*

I'll probably never have children because
I don't believe in touching people for any
reason.

—*Paula Poundstone*

I've been in therapy once a week for sixteen
years. My friend thought that was rather
extensive, so I brought her home to meet my
family. Now she goes twice a week.

—*Cathy Ladman*

[My mother] was afraid of me. I was so
free-spirited, I was hard to control. She
thought something horrible would happen
to me. "You keep doing that and you'll end
up a whore!"

—*Kirstie Alley*

113

I'm a godmother—that's a great thing to be, a godmother. She calls me God for short. That's cute, I taught her that.

—*Ellen DeGeneres*

Three stages in a parent's life: Nutrition, dentition, tuition.

—*Marcelene Cox*

It is true that I was born in Iowa, but I can't speak for my twin sister.

—*Abigail Van Buren*

My mom said she learned how to swim. Someone took her out in the lake and threw her off the boat. That's how she learned to swim. I said, "Mom, they weren't trying to teach you how to swim."

— Paula Poundstone

Fashion and Makeup

Taking joy in life is a woman's best cosmetic.

— Rosalind Russell

Your problem is your role models were models.

— Jane Wagner

Fashion is something that goes in one year and out the other.

— Denise Klahn

I love looking at models—it's hysterical.
I love seeing the British models, especially
the working-class ones who have their
friends from comprehensive schools as
their assistants.

—*Tracey Ullman*

Who said that clothes make a statement? What
an understatement that was. Clothes never
shut up.

—*Susan Brownmiller*

Even when I know it isn't true, some little
part of me always clings to the hope that
everything would be different if I just had
a new color of lipstick.

—*Cathy Guisewite*

I was treated as a coat hanger. Designers don't like breasts and hips because they make bumps in their clothes. It's a way to control women's bodies and their sexuality. But I was very lucky. There was a brief period after Twiggy when somehow normal-size women like Cheryl Tiegs and me were on covers, and we looked like the porkers of all time.

—*Cybill Shepherd*

Brevity is the soul of lingerie.

—*Dorothy Parker*

A woman's dress should be like a barbed-wire fence: serving its purpose without obstructing the view.

—*Sophia Loren*

117

Everyone asked how the dress [I wore to the Emmys] was staying on, so I said there were tiny little helicopters above me and I was attached by a harness. I didn't keep this dress because where am I going to wear it again, Thanksgiving dinner?

—*Julia Louis-Dreyfus*

I dress for women, and undress for men.

—*Angie Dickinson*

Every year I spend thousands of dollars on those dresses [for the Emmys], and the next day they smell of beer and cigarettes from the party, and you can't wear them again.

—*Tracey Ullman*

While clothes with pictures and/or writing
on them are not entirely an invention of the
modern age, they are an unpleasant indication
of the general state of things. . . . I mean, be
realistic. If people don't want to listen to you,
what makes you think they want to hear from
your sweater?

—Fran Lebowitz

Men with pierced ears are better prepared
for marriage—they've experienced pain and
bought jewelry.

—Rita Rudner

Do they take off and fly around the room?

—Emmy Gay, *on supermodels*

So it is all the same day—the past, the present,
and the future existing on the same plane—
but you just have to change your drawers
every couple of hours.

—*Whoopi Goldberg*

I was on a worst-dressed list, which is how
I knew that I was famous. Most people who
don't want to be seen not looking their best go
out in full makeup. But I always want to be
myself. If I'm out and look like this and the
paparazzi are there, I say, "Go right ahead."
I don't run and hide. I'm just trying to be the
same person I was in the beginning.

—*Rosie O'Donnell*

I know there are nights when I have power, when I could put on something and walk in somewhere, and if there is a man who doesn't look at me, it's because he's gay.

—*Kathleen Turner*

I began wearing hats as a young lawyer because it helped me to establish my professional identity. Before that, whenever I was at a meeting, someone would ask me to get coffee—they assumed I was a secretary.

—*Bella Abzug*

You can say what you like about long dresses, but they cover a multitude of shins.

—*Mae West*

Everything sets people up for competition these days. All the advertising. I don't know what they do. They sit in these rooms and they think up this stuff. It's insane. "All right, let's think of some new names for these perfumes! Okay, you're really in competition with your best friend. You covet everything she has. You're jealous. You're bitter. You even want her husband. You're a backstabbing bitch. Envy by Gucci. Yes!"

—*Sandra Bernhard*

You'd be surprised how much it costs to look this cheap.

—*Dolly Parton*

Fur used to turn heads, now it turns stomachs.
— *Rue McClanahan*

Seamed stockings aren't subtle but they certainly do the job. You shouldn't wear them when out with someone you're not prepared to sleep with, since their presence is tantamount to saying, "Hi there, big fellow, please rip my clothes off at your earliest opportunity." If you really want your escort paralytic with lust, stop frequently to adjust the seams.
— *Cynthia Heimel*

If the shoe fits, it's too expensive.
— *Adrienne Gusoff*

I base
most of my
fashion sense
on what
doesn't itch.

—Gilda Radner

My husband gave me a necklace. It's fake.
I requested fake. Maybe I'm paranoid, but
in this day and age, I don't want something
around my neck that's worth more than
my head.

—*Rita Rudner*

Designer clothes worn by children are like
snowsuits worn by adults. Few can carry it
off successfully.

—*Fran Lebowitz*

Any garment that makes you feel bad will
make you look bad.

—*Victoria Billings*

If men can run the world, why can't they stop wearing neckties? How intelligent is it to start the day by tying a little noose around your neck?

— *Linda Ellerbee*

Feminism and Women's Liberation

These are very confusing times. For the first time in history a woman is expected to combine intelligence with a sharp hairdo, a raised consciousness with high heels, and an open, nonsexist relationship with a tan guy who has a great bod.

— *Lynda Barry*

I'm tired of earning my own living, paying my own bills, raising my own child. I'm tired of the sound of my own voice crying out in the wilderness, raving on about equality and justice and a new social order. . . . Self-sufficiency is exhausting. Autonomy is lonely. It's so hard to be a feminist if you're a woman.

—*Jane O'Reilly*

The women's movement hasn't changed my sex life. It wouldn't dare.

—*Zsa Zsa Gabor*

I wanted to be the first woman to burn her bra, but it would have taken the fire department four days to put it out.

—*Dolly Parton*

I remember when women's lib started happening, this article came out that chopped me up for being this . . . nitwit. I never looked at myself as a nitwit. I never looked at anything I did as vacant or dumb or bubbleheaded. There was always a sensibility about what I did. Because someone has an optimistic outlook, because someone is hopeful, because someone likes to have fun, because someone is trusting and open, does not necessarily mean that someone is stupid.

—Goldie Hawn

I'm glad we feminists don't have to burn our bras anymore because the Wonderbra would never go out. You could use it for the Olympic torch.

—Emmy Gay

Yes, it's a man's world, but that's all right because they're making a total mess of it. We're chipping away at their control, taking the parts we want. Some women think it's a difficult task, but it's not.

— *Cher*

I'm furious about the Women's Liberationists. They keep getting up on soapboxes and proclaiming that women are brighter than men. That's true, but it should be kept very quiet or it ruins the whole racket.

—*Anita Loos*

Food, Dieting, and Exercise

I don't work out. If God wanted us to bend
over, he'd put diamonds on the floor.

—Joan Rivers

The only reason I would take up jogging is
so I could hear heavy breathing again.

—Erma Bombeck

The day is divided into two important sections:
Mealtime and everything else.

—Merrill Markoe

Where do you go to get anorexia?

—Shelley Winters

I have gained and lost the same ten pounds so many times over and over again my cellulite must have déjà vu.

—*Jane Wagner*

I was a vegetarian until I started leaning toward sunlight.

—*Rita Rudner*

Women should try to increase their size rather than decrease it, because I believe the bigger we are, the more space we'll take up, and the more we'll have to be reckoned with.

—*Roseanne*

Food is an important part of a balanced diet.

—*Fran Lebowitz*

Did you ever get somethin' stuck in your teeth and you didn't know what the heck it was?

—*Gilda Radner*

Keep fit–but not for your men. Do it for yourselves.

—*Jane Fonda*

This is a law in America, that you have to have sugar, brown sugar, the chemical companies have to be represented. You must have the ones that cause cancer, [and] the ones that don't cause cancer.

—*Tracey Ullman*

Salad isn't food. Salad is slimy green background for croutons.

—*Cynthia Heimel*

I've been on a diet for two weeks and all I've lost is two weeks.

—*Totie Fields*

Ever notice that Soup for One is eight aisles away from party mix?

—*Elayne Boosler*

My favorite animal is steak.

—*Fran Lebowitz*

There's a territorial ritual to an aerobics class. I entered a class for the first time a few years ago and ended up where no one wanted to be . . . in the front row next to the mirror. It was three years before I could work my way to the back row.

— Erma Bombeck

I plan on using more common sense in the future when it comes to my eating habits. More fruit and vegetables. I don't eat much meat, fish, or poultry. After all, you never know what they are doing to the water and all the other stuff.

— Carol Burnett

I did try to give up coffee once. We were playing in Dayton, Ohio, and I went totally blank onstage. My leading man, Jay Garner, gave me my line. Then it happened again, and he helped me again. I kept forgetting where we were in the show. Finally, I said to the audience, "Look, the problem with this scene is I've given up coffee. If you are on coffee, don't try to get off of it." With that, the drummer, Joe DeLuca, rose up in the pit and handed me a cup of coffee. I took a drink and said, "I'll never give it up again." The audience loved it; I think they thought it was part of the show.

— *Carol Channing*

I am not a glutton—I am an explorer of food.
— *Erma Bombeck*

Never eat more than you can lift.

—*Miss Piggy*

I'm going to the StairMaster ring of Dante's Inferno, because I hate the damn machine so much. I do it on manual, so I can control it. But I don't put my hands on the rails, so I can keep a good flow going. That way it's two annoying workouts in one.

—*Janeane Garofalo, when asked by Playboy magazine where we go when we die*

I like winter because I can stay indoors without feeling guilty.

—*Teressa Skelton*

I'm not into working out. My philosophy:
No pain, no pain.

—*Carol Leifer*

Breakfast cereals that come in the same colors
as polyester leisure suits make oversleeping
a virtue.

—*Fran Lebowitz*

I prefer Hostess fruit pies to pop-up toaster
tarts because they don't require so much
cooking.

—*Carrie Snow*

They put me in a crib with two sides and cut
my leg off. How was I to get to a refrigerator?

—*Totie Fields*

137

Cooked Carrots: On way to mouth, drop in lap. Smuggle to garbage in napkin.

—*Delia Ephron*

I don't even butter my bread. I consider that cooking.

—*Katherine Cebrian*

Because there does not seem to be anything around to eat certainly does not mean there is nothing to eat. . . . Don't discount things which are mouth-size because you cannot identify them. These things can, and should, be considered as gum.

—*Merrill Markoe*

Research tells us that fourteen out of any ten individuals like chocolate.

—*Sandra Boynton*

Those magazine dieting stories always have the testimonial of a woman who wore a dress that could slipcover New Jersey in one photo and thirty days later looked like a well-dressed thermometer.

— *Erma Bombeck*

Everything you see I owe to spaghetti.

— *Sophia Loren*

If you knew how meat was made, you'd probably lose your lunch. I'm from cattle country. That's why I became a vegetarian.

— *k.d. lang*

Friends and Enemies

I can trust my friends. . . . These people force me to examine myself, encourage me to grow.
— *Cher*

[Friendships] are easy to get out of compared to love affairs, but they are not easy to get out of compared to, say, jail.
— *Fran Lebowitz*

Sometimes you have to get to know someone really well to realize you're really strangers.
— *Mary Tyler Moore*

Four be the things I am wiser to know:
Idleness, sorrow, a friend, and a foe.

—Dorothy Parker

Jane [Curtin] lives up the street. I see her
walking her dog. We flip each other off and
stuff and then laugh.

—Laraine Newman on her fellow
Saturday Night Live former class member

She's so fat she's my two best friends. She
wears stretch caftans. She's got more chins
than the Chinese telephone directory.

—Joan Rivers

I can get along with anybody . . . provided
they're fat.

—Susan Richman

The more I traveled the more I realized that
fear makes strangers of people who should
be friends.

—*Shirley MacLaine*

I've never hated a man enough to give him
his diamonds back.

—*Zsa Zsa Gabor*

Gender Gap

When women get depressed, they eat or go
shopping. Men invade another country. It's a
whole different way of thinking.

—*Elayne Boosler*

FUNNY LADIES

We live in a sexist society, and men automatically command more respect when they walk out onstage. As a woman, you walk out there and everyone hushes. "Ah, she thinks she's funny. What can you do to make me laugh?" They don't do that to a man. They are eager and ready, and he has to prove he's not funny before they give him the ice treatment. Women have to constantly win them over.

— Kim Wayans

Women are so inconsequential in society that nobody knows what our stuff is called. The cervix. You ask 95 percent of the people on the street, "Where's the cervix?" and they turn around and point to the top of their neck.

— Reno (Karen Renaud)

Still, if we were back at the table, I'd probably have to talk to him. Look at him—what could you say to a thing like that? Did you go to the circus this year, what's your favorite kind of ice cream, how do you spell *cat*? I guess I'm as well off here. As well off as if I were in a cement mixer in full action.

—Dorothy Parker

When Venus said, "Spell *no* for me,"
"N-O" Dan Cupid wrote with glee,
And smiled at his success:
"Ah, child," said Venus, laughing low,
"We women do not spell it so,
We spell it Y-E-S."

—Carolyn Wells, "The Spelling Lesson"

I do not know who first invented the myth of sexual equality. But it is a myth willfully fostered and nourished by certain semiscientists and other fiction writers. And it has done more, I suspect, to unsettle marital happiness than any other false doctrine of this myth-ridden age.

—*Phyllis McGinley*

Sometimes I wonder if men and women really suit each other. Perhaps they should live next door and just visit now and then.

—*Katharine Hepburn*

A man has every season while a woman only has the right to spring.

—*Jane Fonda*

If you kept seeing Robert Redford stark naked on the screen, would he be a superstar today? No way. Or Gene Hackman showing everything? Their million-dollar days would be over. I want to be in a movie where all the men take their clothes off and I don't.

—*Cybill Shepherd*

A man can sleep around, no questions asked, but if a woman makes nineteen or twenty mistakes she's a tramp.

—*Joan Rivers*

When a man gets hanged, he gets an erection, but when a woman gets hanged, the *last* thing on her mind is sex.

—*Jane Wagner*

It is a known fact that men are practical,
hardheaded realists, in contrast to women,
who are romantic dreamers and actually
believe that estrogenic skin cream must do
something or they couldn't charge sixteen
dollars for that little jar.

—*Jane Goodsell*

I never realized until lately that women were
supposed to be the inferior sex.

—*Katharine Hepburn*

Men think their version of reality is *the* Reality.
I like my version of reality to be dominant.

—*Kim Wayans*

Now men and women are separate but unequal. We should be hand in hand; in fact, we should have our arms around each other.

— *Cloris Leachman*

We've got a generation now who were born with semiequality. They don't know how it was before, so they think, This isn't too bad. We're working. We have our attaché cases and our three-piece suits. I get very disgusted with the younger generation of women. We had a torch to pass, and they are just sitting there. They don't realize it can be taken away. Things are going to have to get worse before they join in fighting the battle.

— *Erma Bombeck*

I can't believe that anyone would still have a problem with women being funny. What century is that? I guess they're the same people who think that a football player can't do needlepoint or take ballet. I don't know who those people are, but I don't want them in my audience.

—Ellen DeGeneres

Women speak because they wish to speak, whereas a man speaks only when driven to speech by something outside himself—like, for instance, he can't find any clean socks.

—Jean Kerr

One of my theories is that men love with their eyes; women love with their ears.

—Zsa Zsa Gabor

The woman's position in the world today is so much harder than a man's that it makes me choke every time I hear a man complain about anything.

—Katharine Hepburn

A man who graduated high in his class at Yale Law School and made partnership in a top law firm would be celebrated. A man who invested wisely would be admired, but a woman who accomplishes this is treated with suspicion.

—Barbra Streisand

Happiness

We're all pursuing happiness. What I learned
is that every moment is not a living hell; we're
happier than we realize. We just don't know it.
—*Merrill Markoe*

It is only possible to live happily ever after on
a day-to-day basis.
—*Margaret Bonnano*

What a lovely surprise to discover how
unlonely being alone can be.
—*Ellen Burstyn*

A sure way to lose happiness, I found, is to want it at the expense of everything else.
—*Bette Davis*

If you always do what interests you, at least one person is pleased.
—*Katharine Hepburn*

No matter how lonely you get or how many birth announcements you receive, the trick is not to get frightened. There's nothing wrong with being alone.
—*Wendy Wasserstein*

If a day goes by and I haven't been slain,
I'm happy.

—*Carol Leifer*

People used to ask me what I wanted to be
when I grew up, and I'd say, "Happy!" That
was all I wanted to be.

—*Goldie Hawn*

We have lived through the era when happiness
was a warm puppy, and the era when happiness was a dry martini, and now we have
come to the era when happiness is knowing
what your uterus looks like.

—*Nora Ephron*

Human Nature

I never like anyone till I've seen him at
his worst.

—*Ethel May Dell*

You can fool all of the people some of the
time, and some of the people all of the time.
And that's sufficient.

—*Rose King*

Guilt: The gift that keeps on giving.

—*Erma Bombeck*

Normal is in the eye of the beholder.

—*Whoopi Goldberg*

Each of us only feels the torn lining of his own coat and sees the wholeness of the other person's.

— *Erica Jong*

What is sauce for the goose may be sauce for the gander, but it is not necessarily sauce for the chicken, the duck, the turkey, or the guinea hen.

—*Alice B. Toklas*

The statistics on sanity are that one out of every four Americans is suffering from some form of mental illness. Think of your three best friends. If they're okay, then it's you.

—*Rita Mae Brown*

Maybe being oneself is always an acquired taste.
— *Patricia Hampl*

Revenge leads to an empty fullness, like eating dirt.
— *Mignon McLaughlin*

In our country they love to build people up— and smash them.
— *Florence Henderson*

I have my standards. They may be low, but I have them.
— *Bette Midler*

A bore is a person not interested in you.
— *Mary Pettibone Poole*

Humor and Laughter

There's a hell of a distance between wise-cracking and wit. Wit has truth in it; wise-cracking is simply calisthenics with words.
— Dorothy Parker

The person who knows how to laugh at himself will never cease to be amused.
— Shirley MacLaine

Normal is just a cycle on the washing machine.
— Whoopi Goldberg

An onion can make you cry, but show me the vegetable that can make you laugh!

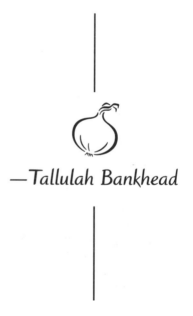

—Tallulah Bankhead

Being a funny person does an awful lot of things to you. You feel that you mustn't get serious with people. They don't expect it from you, and they don't want to see it. You're not entitled to be serious, you're a clown, and they only want you to make them laugh.

—*Fanny Brice*

He who laughs last didn't get it.

—*Helen Giangregorio*

There are so few Methodist comics, don't you know? They do a few dinner jokes and go away.

—*Kate Clinton*

When humor goes, there goes civilization.
—*Erma Bombeck*

Laughter is a strange response. I mean, what is it? It's a spasm of some kind! Is that always joy? It's very often discomfort. It's some sort of explosive reaction.
—*Madeline Kahn*

Comedy is tragedy plus time.
—*Carol Burnett*

That is the best—to laugh with someone because you think the same things are funny.
—*Gloria Vanderbilt*

161

Comedy is harder to do [than drama]. It's very hard to make people laugh. It's like a soufflé—if it gets overdone, the soufflé crashes. That's how delicate comedy is. Comedy is like music. I remember working with an actor who couldn't get the scene, couldn't get the timing. So I beat it out on my hands. It was like percussion, so he could understand the arch of the scene and the power that it had to have. It's as if I hear the beats in my head.

—*Goldie Hawn*

He who laughs, lasts.

—*Mary Pettibone Poole*

Rule One: Never go onstage until the audience pledges to give you all their worldly possessions. It makes them feel needed. Rule Two: If an audience is unusually quiet—or, as I would say, hopelessly stupid—try something different . . . like a joke of your own. Rule Three: If a cigar-chomping club owner who used to run a strip joint tells you how to do your act, just politely say, "Hey, Sponge, why not stick to your own job, which is to cheat me out of as much money as possible." Rule Four: Never let the audience reshape your head during a performance, especially if it improves the show. Rule Five: If all else fails, learn to juggle.

—*Judy Tenuta, on her rules of stand-up comedy*

I hate all that "Ladies, back me up on this" kind of humor. I'm trying to portray a strong, single woman in the nineties, which I am in real life. But I don't think that I act or behave anything like how a thirty-seven-year-old woman is supposed to act. I really think of myself as a girl, not a woman. I know some women will be offended, but I just feel it's a matter of redefining our sex.

— *Ellen DeGeneres*

Inadvertently Amusing

Right now, I'm a freshman in my fourth year at UCLA, but my goal is to become a veterinarian, 'cause I love children.

— *Julie Brown*

Fiction writing is great. You can make up almost anything.

— *Ivana Trump*

I want all hellions to quit puffing that hell fume in God's clean air.

— *Carry Nation, on smoking*

The art of pressing flowers is as relevant today as it was one hundred years ago.

— *Martha Stewart*

Whenever I watch TV and see those poor starving kids all over the world, I can't help but cry. I mean I'd love to be skinny like that but not with all those flies and death and stuff.

— *Mariah Carey*

Being popular is important. Otherwise people might not like you.

—*Mimi Pond*

How did I feel when I first got the call that I was booked for *Sports Illustrated*? . . . I don't know, I mean, um . . . how did Louie Armstrong feel when he first walked on the moon?

—*Rebecca Romijin-Stamos*

I believe that mink are raised for being turned into fur coats, and if we didn't wear fur coats those little animals would never have been born. So is it better not to have been born or to have lived for a year or two to have been turned into a fur coat? I don't know.

—*Barbi Benton*

Smoking kills. If you're killed, you've lost a very important part of your life.

—Brooke Shields

I catnap now and then, but I think while
I nap, so it's not a waste of time.

—*Martha Stewart*

Life Lessons

I made some studies, and reality is the leading
cause of stress amongst those in touch with it.
I can take it in small doses, but as a lifestyle,
I found it too confining.

—*Jane Wagner*

Life is something to do when you can't get to
sleep.

—*Fran Lebowitz*

Reality is just a crutch for people who can't cope with drugs.

— *Lily Tomlin*

Experience is a good teacher, but she sends in terrific bills.

— *Minna Antrim*

At the moment you are most in awe of all there is about life that you don't understand, you are closer to understanding it all than at any other time.

— *Jane Wagner*

I finally figured out the only reason to be alive is to enjoy it.

— *Rita Mae Brown*

Most of us live our lives devoid of cinematic
moments.
— *Nora Ephron*

If you're not living on the edge, you're taking
up too much room.
— *Lorraine Teel*

No matter how big or soft your bed is, you
still have to get out of it.
— *Grace Slick*

Our ability to delude ourselves may be an
important survival tool.
— *Jane Wagner*

It has begun to occur to me that life is a stage I'm going through.

— *Ellen Goodman*

No matter how cynical you become, it's never enough to keep up.

— *Lily Tomlin*

I have always been driven by some distant music—a battle hymn no doubt—for I have been at war from the beginning. I've never looked back before. I've never had the time and it has always seemed so dangerous. To look back is to relax one's vigil.

— *Bette Davis*

My greatest enemy is reality. I have fought it successfully for thirty years.

—*Margaret Anderson*

Only dead fish swim with the stream.

—*Linda Ellerbee*

Experience: A comb life gives you after you lose your hair.

—*Judith Stern*

I think we're here for each other.

—*Carol Burnett*

Reality is something you rise above.

—*Liza Minnelli*

I've learned that if you know that you are giving all that you can give, and it still doesn't make the difference, you must give up control over others. The only person that you can control in the whole entire universe is yourself. Other than that, you might as well throw in the towel early.

—*Goldie Hawn*

Everybody wants to do something to help, but nobody wants to be the first.

—*Pearl Bailey, on change*

The average, healthy, well-adjusted adult gets up at seven-thirty in the morning feeling just plain terrible.

—*Jean Kerr*

Reality is nothing but a collective hunch.
— Lily Tomlin

Men always fall for frigid women because they put on the best show.
— Fanny Brice

Egotism—usually just a case of mistaken nonentity.
— Barbara Stanwyck

Humility is no substitute for a good personality.
— Fran Lebowitz

Mothers, food, love, and career: The four major guilt groups.
— Cathy Guisewite

I cannot and will not cut my conscience to fit this year's fashions.

— *Lillian Hellman*

A sobering thought: What if, right at this very moment, I am living up to my full potential?

— *Jane Wagner*

We're just God's way of playing Monopoly. Think of your life and the people and the struggle, and God's sitting up there eating popcorn and having a laugh at it all.

— *Marsha Warfield*

Compromise, if not the spice of life, is its solidity.

— *Phyllis McGinley*

175

I wanted a perfect ending. Now I've learned, the hard way, that some poems don't rhyme, and some stories don't have a clear beginning, middle, and end. Life is about not knowing, having to change, taking the moment and making the best of it, without knowing what's going to happen next. Delicious ambiguity.

—Gilda Radner

I've never looked through a keyhole without finding someone was looking back.

—Judy Garland

We don't stop going to school when we graduate.

—Carol Burnett

I'm the foe of moderation, the champion of excess. If I may lift a line from a diehard whose identity is lost in the shuffle, "I'd rather be strongly wrong than weakly right."

—*Tallulah Bankhead*

I've learned how to make deals. I've learned how to negotiate and that some things are more important than others. In order to get what you want, you have to choose what's important. You have to find the point past which you would never go. I've learned how to take responsibility for what comes on my watch. You know the old expression, "It happened on my watch"? Well, you have to take responsibility. And I've learned where to buy my bras.

—*Bette Midler*

Hope is the feeling you have that the feeling
you have isn't permanent.

—*Jean Kerr*

Procrastination gives you something to look
forward to.

—*Joan Konner*

Everybody knows that if you are too careful
you are so occupied in being careful that you
are sure to stumble over something.

—*Gertrude Stein*

One learns in life to keep silent and draw
one's own confusions.

—*Cornelia Otis Skinner*

The weak are the most treacherous of us all.
They come to the strong and drain them.
They are bottomless. They are insatiable.
They are always parched and always bitter.
They are everyone's concern, and like
vampires they suck our life's blood.

— *Bette Davis*

I think I'm here for a reason. And I think a
little bit of the reason is to throw little torches
out to the next step to lead people through the
dark. When you're kind to someone in trouble
you hope they'll remember to be kind to
someone else.

— *Whoopi Goldberg*

Once you can laugh at your own weaknesses, you can move forward. Comedy breaks down walls. It opens up people. If you're good, you can fill up those openings with something positive. Maybe you can combat some of the ugliness in the world.

—*Goldie Hawn*

Our lives are like soap operas. We can go for months and not tune in to them, then six months later we look in and the same stuff is going on.

—*Jane Wagner*

Not only is life a bitch, it has puppies.

—*Adrienne Gusoff*

My parents are insane; three kitchen chairs pushed together can make an excellent bed; holidays are no time to visit the family; "rotate the tires" means moving them to different wheels; most people on welfare couldn't plan far enough ahead to scam the government, even if they want to; I am insane.

— *Paula Poundstone*

Self-confidence: When you think that your greatest fault is being too hard on yourself.

— *Judith Viorst*

Parables are unnecessary for recognizing the blatant absurdity of everyday life. Reality is lesson enough.

— *Jane O'Reilly*

It's such an act of optimism to get through
a day and enjoy it and laugh and do all that
without thinking about death. What spirit
human beings have!

—*Gilda Radner*

Life is hard. After all, it kills you.

—*Katharine Hepburn*

If I've learned one thing in life it's Listen
to yourself. The one thing I can't stand:
Someone talking to me when I'm sleeping.
Three words that best describe me:
A regular person.

—*Ellen Cleghorne*

The wrong people are in charge. Especially in America. That the people you thought knew what they were doing—doctors, scientists, politicians, lawyers, pilots—don't. That they're as stupid as you and I are, which is frightening. That educated people aren't necessarily clever. That there are no more rain forests nor ozone layer. That we're all going to die. That there are no bargains anywhere. That the Pinewood condos in Palm Springs are no match for the south of France. That you're never going to get a decent perm if you do it at home. And that the best thing to do in life is laugh.

—*Tracey Ullman*

Love

Sex is an emotion in motion. . . . Love is what you make it and who you make it with.

—*Mae West*

Love is a fire. But whether it is going to warm your hearth or burn down your house, you can never tell.

—*Joan Crawford*

Love yourself first and everything else falls into line. You really have to love yourself to get anything done in this world.

—*Lucille Ball*

Love for me is
like a pretzel.
Twisted and
salty.

—Emmy Gay

The sweetest joy, the wildest woe is love.
— *Pearl Bailey*

Love is the only shocking act left on the face of the earth.
— *Sandra Bernhard*

Love is much nicer to be in than an automobile accident, a tight girdle, a higher tax bracket, or a holding pattern over Philadelphia.
— *Judith Viorst*

When you are in love with someone you want to be near him all the time, except when you are out buying things and charging them to him.
— *Miss Piggy*

If it is your time love will track you like a cruise missile. If you say, "No! I don't want it right now," that's when you'll get it for sure. Love will make a way out of no way. Love is an exploding cigar which we willingly smoke.
— *Lynda Barry*

Love is a narcissism shared by two.
— *Rita Mae Brown*

In the arithmetic of love, one plus one equals everything and two minus one equals nothing.
— *Mignon McLaughlin*

What the world really needs is more love and less paperwork.
— *Pearl Bailey*

If love is the answer, could you please
rephrase the question?

— *Lily Tomlin*

Infatuation is when you think that he's as
sexy as Robert Redford, as smart as Henry
Kissinger, as noble as Ralph Nader, as funny
as Woody Allen, and as athletic as Jimmy
Connors. Love is when you realize that he's
as sexy as Woody Allen, as smart as Jimmy
Connors, as funny as Ralph Nader, as athletic
as Henry Kissinger, and nothing like Robert
Redford — but you'll take him anyway.

—*Judith Viorst*

Love is like playing checkers. You have to
know which man to move.

—*Jackie "Moms" Mabley*

When you love somebody, you look at him
sometimes and think, God, I'd die if something ever happened to you or if you left.
I'd be devastated. And that's not such a bad
feeling. One shouldn't be so afraid of that,
because a lot of times, people don't get
involved with that kind of deep love because
they're so afraid of losing it. So they lose it.
At least they had it.

—*Goldie Hawn*

Love conquers all things except poverty and
toothache.

—*Mae West*

Love is a game that two can play and both win.

—*Eva Gabor*

189

Despite everything that had happened to me,
I still expected that one day I would fall in
love even though I had no idea what that was.
I watched everyone to see if I could see it.
But I don't think that love lived in my neigh-
borhood, or if it did, there was nothing pretty
about it. Made me wonder why everyone
wanted to fall.

— *Robin Quivers*

Love, the quest; marriage, the conquest;
divorce, the inquest.

— *Helen Rowland*

Marriage and Divorce

When a man brings his wife flowers for no reason—there's a reason.

—*Molly McGee*

It seemed to me that the desire to get married—which, I regret to say, I believe is basic and primal in women—is followed almost immediately by an equally basic and primal urge—which is to be single again.

—*Nora Ephron*

Divorce: Fission after fusion.

—*Rita Mae Brown*

191

I've never been married, but I tell people I'm divorced so they won't think something's wrong with me.

—*Elayne Boosler*

My husband will never chase another woman. He's too fine, too decent, too old.

—*Gracie Allen*

I was married for seventeen years, and I couldn't pick out his face in a police lineup. I can't even remember his face.

—*Joy Behar*

A man is incomplete until he has married. Then he's finished.

—*Zsa Zsa Gabor*

Why does a woman work ten years to change
a man's habits and then complain that he's not
the man she married?

—Barbra Streisand

I used to believe that marriage would diminish
me, reduce my options. That you had to be
someone less to live with someone else when,
of course, you have to be someone more.

—Candice Bergen

I'd marry again if I found a man who had
fifteen million and would sign over half of it
to me before the marriage and guarantee he'd
be dead within a year.

—Bette Davis

Divorce is defeat.

—Lucille Ball

Marrying a man is like buying something you've been admiring for a long time in a shop window. You may love it when you get it home, but it doesn't always go with everything else.

—Jean Kerr

Marriage is a great institution, but I'm not ready for an institution.

—Mae West

Whatever you may look like, marry a man your own age—as your beauty fades, so will his eyesight.

—Phyllis Diller

The doctor must have put my pacemaker in wrong. Every time my husband kisses me, the garage door goes up.

—*Minnie Pearl*

He tricked me into marrying him. He told me I was pregnant.

—*Carol Leifer*

Being divorced is like being hit by a Mack truck. If you live through it, you start looking very carefully to the right and to the left.

—*Jean Kerr*

I get upset when guys I don't know see other women.

—*Cathy Ladman*

[My husband and I] have a saying in our house: If I wanted you to be the devil, I would have married the devil.

—*Kirstie Alley*

Husbands are like fires. They go out when unattended.

—*Zsa Zsa Gabor*

No man worth his salt, no man of spirit and spine, no man for whom I could have any respect, could rejoice in the identification of Tallulah's husband. It's tough enough to be bogged down in a legend. It would be even tougher to marry one.

—*Tallulah Bankhead*

A husband is what is left of the lover after the nerve has been extracted.

—*Helen Rowland*

Whenever you want to marry someone, go have lunch with his ex-wife.

—*Shelley Winters*

I earn and pay my own way as a great many women do today. Why should unmarried women be discriminated against—unmarried men are not.

—*Dinah Shore*

I've had diseases that lasted longer than my marriages.

—*Nell Carter*

If love means never having to say you're sorry, then marriage means always having to say everything twice.

—*Estelle Getty*

I love being married. It's so great to find that one special person you want to annoy for the rest of your life.

—*Rita Rudner*

All marriages are happy. It's trying to live together afterwards that causes all the problems.

—*Shelley Winters*

It was so cold I almost got married.

—*Shelley Winters*

You may marry the man of your dreams, ladies, but fourteen years later you're married to a couch that burps.

—*Roseanne*

I suppose when they reach a certain age some men are afraid to grow up. It seems the older the men get, the younger their new wives get.

—*Elizabeth Taylor*

Marriage is too interesting an experiment to be tried only once.

—*Eva Gabor*

It was a mixed marriage: I'm human. He's a Klingon.

—*Carol Leifer*

199

How many husbands have I had? You mean apart from my own?

—Zsa Zsa Gabor

If you want to sacrifice the admiration of many men for the criticism of one, go ahead, get married.

—Katharine Hepburn

I've married a few people I shouldn't have, but haven't we all?

—Mamie Van Doren

The trouble with some women is that they get all excited about nothing—and then marry him.

—Cher

I married the first man I ever kissed. When I tell this to my children they just about throw up.

— *Barbara Bush*

Is there a doctor in the house? My parents want me to marry you.

— *Wendy Liebman*

My boyfriend and I broke up. He wanted to get married, and I didn't want him to.

— *Rita Rudner*

My husband and I didn't sign a prenuptial agreement. We signed a mutual suicide pact.

— *Roseanne*

FUNNY LADIES

When you see what some girls marry,
you realize how they must hate to work
for a living.

—Helen Rowland

I can't mate in captivity.

—Gloria Steinem, on being asked
why she hadn't married

It is true that I never should have married,
but I didn't want to live without a man.
Brought up to respect the conventions, love
had to end in marriage. I'm afraid it did.

—Bette Davis

Media

Never joke with the press. Irony does not translate into newsprint.

—*Erica Jong*

You should always believe what you read in the newspapers, for that makes them more interesting.

—*Rose Macauley*

Everybody gets so much common information all day long that they lose their common sense.

—*Gertrude Stein*

With publicity comes humiliation.

—*Tama Janowitz*

If Sigmund Freud had watched Phil Donahue
he would never have wondered what women
want.

— *Nora Ephron*

A bad review is like baking a cake with all the
best ingredients and having someone sit on it.

— *Danielle Steel*

Death will be a great relief. No more interviews.

— *Katharine Hepburn*

Radio news is bearable. This is due to the
fact that while the news is being broadcast,
the disc jockey is not allowed to talk.

— *Fran Lebowitz*

Here I am, one of the most colorful women of my time—if not of my block—being made to sound positively legumelike in printed interviews.

—Bette Midler

Mistakes and Regrets

The only thing I regret about my life is the length of it. If I had to live my life again, I'd make all the same mistakes—only sooner.

—Tallulah Bankhead

If every single thing goes well for me from this day forward and I live twice as long and hit eighty, I still screwed up at least half of my life.

—Merrill Markoe

To err is human—but it feels divine.

—Mae West

You take your life in your own hands, and what happens? A terrible thing: No one to blame.

—Erica Jong

Telling lies and showing off to get attention are mistakes I made that I don't want my kids to make.

—Jane Fonda

Keep a diary and one day it'll keep you.

—Mae West

People are so busy dreaming the American Dream, fantasizing about what they could be or have a right to be, that they're all asleep at the switch. Consequently we are living in the Age of Human Error.

—Florence King

If I could change one thing about myself, I'd be younger. I'd love to start over.

—Ellen Cleghorne

I always wanted to be somebody, but I should have been more specific.

—Lily Tomlin

Motherhood and Pregnancy

A child of one can be taught not to do certain
things, such as touch a hot stove, turn on the
gas, pull lamps off their tables by their cords,
or wake Mommy before noon.

—*Joan Rivers*

If pregnancy were a book they would cut the
last two chapters.

—*Nora Ephron*

Sometimes when I look at my children,
I say to myself, "Lillian, you should have
stayed a virgin."

—*Lillian Carter, mother of Jimmy and Billy*

Sex is still the leading cause of pregnancy.

—Frederica
Mathewes-Green

The biggest lesson we have to give our children is truth. And that's what I'm saying: That we're all built with illusions. And they break.

— *Goldie Hawn*

Our bodies are shaped to bear children, and our lives are a working out of the processes of creation. All our ambitions and intelligence are beside that great elemental point.

— *Phyllis McGinley*

Giving birth is like taking your lower lip and forcing it over your head.

— *Carol Burnett*

I figure that if the children are alive when I get home, I've done my job.

— *Roseanne*

Every now and then I feel a little bit bad for Joan Crawford. It's not like I condone child abuse. But I think the story is told so one-sided that it makes it look as if one night there was a mistake with wire hangers. What they don't show is the buildup to that where she said a million times, "Hey, don't use wire hangers." Why they should choose that one peccadillo, I don't know.

— *Paula Poundstone*

There's a lot more to being a woman than being a mother, but there's a hell of a lot more to being a mother than most people suspect.

— *Roseanne*

Dear Mary: We all knew you had it in you.

— *Dorothy Parker, in a telegram to a friend who had given birth*

Envy the kangaroo. The pouch setup is extraordinary; the baby crawls out of the womb when it is about two inches long, gets into the pouch, and proceeds to mature. I'd have a baby if it would develop in my handbag.

— *Rita Rudner*

My obstetrician was so dumb that when I gave birth he forgot to cut the cord. For a year that kid followed me everywhere. It was like having a dog on a leash.

—*Joan Rivers*

One thing they never tell you about child raising is that for the rest of your life, at the drop of a hat, you are expected to know your child's name and how old he or she is.

—*Erma Bombeck*

You see much more of your children once they leave home.

—*Lucille Ball*

I love my kids, but I wouldn't want them for friends.

—*Janet Sorensen*

I'm not interested in being Wonder Woman in the delivery room. Give me drugs.

—*Madonna*

If God were a woman, She would have installed one of those turkey thermometers in our belly buttons. When we were done, the thermometer pops up, the doctor reaches for the zipper conveniently located beneath our bikini lines, and out comes a smiling, fully diapered baby.

—*Candice Bergen*

One of the things I've discovered in general about raising kids is that they really don't give a damn if you walked five miles to school. They want to deal with what's happening now.

—*Patty Duke*

To me, life is tough enough without having someone kick you from the inside.

—*Rita Rudner*

It actually says on the inside label of the Gerber food jar not to feed the kid out of the jar because it's unappetizing. Unappetizing? Have they seen that food? The strained green beans weren't exactly calling out to me to begin with!

—*Paula Poundstone*

Never lend your car to anyone to whom you have given birth.

—*Erma Bombeck*

I'm like a chimpanzee. I believe kids should stay with their mother for a very long time.

—*Kirstie Alley*

Hard labor: A redundancy, like "working mother."

—*Joyce Armor*

The real menace in dealing with a five-year-old is that in no time at all you begin to sound like a five-year-old.

—*Jean Kerr*

No matter how old a mother is, she watches her middle-aged children for signs of improvement.

— *Florida Scott-Maxwell*

I want to have children, and I know my time is running out; I want to have them while my parents are still young enough to take care of them.

— *Rita Rudner*

My children always had an unusual diet. . . . In general, they refused to eat anything that hadn't danced on TV.

— *Erma Bombeck*

I just can't get over how much babies cry.
I really had no idea what I was getting into.
To tell you the truth, I thought it would be
more like getting a cat.

—*Anne Lamott*

Parties and Other Social Gatherings

If you don't show up at a party, people will
assume you're fat.

—*Stephanie Vanderkellen*

Partying is such sweet sorrow.

—*Jean Kerr*

Just because I have rice on my clothes doesn't mean I've been to a wedding. A Chinese man threw up on me.

— *Phyllis Diller*

What's nice about my dating life is that I don't have to leave my house. All I have to do is read the paper: I'm marrying Richard Gere, dating Daniel Day-Lewis, parading around with John F. Kennedy, Jr., and even Robert De Niro was in there for a day.

— *Julia Roberts*

The cocktail party is easily the worst invention since castor oil.

— *Elsa Maxwell*

Who could deny that privacy is a jewel? It has always been the mark of privilege, the distinguishing feature of a truly urbane culture. Out of the cave, the tribal tepee, the pueblo, the community fortress, man emerged to build himself a house of his own with a shelter in it for himself and his diversions. Every age has seen it so. The poor might have to huddle together in cities for need's sake, and the frontiersman cling to his neighbors for the sake of protection. But in each civilization, as it advanced, those who could afford it chose the luxury of a withdrawing-place.

— *Phyllis McGinley*

Nothing spoils a party like a genius.

— *Elsa Maxwell*

We are all born charming, fresh, and sponta-
neous and must be civilized before we are fit
to participate in society.
—*Judith Martin, Miss Manners*

I went to a literary gathering once. . . . The
place was filled with people who looked as if
they had been scraped up out of the drains.
The ladies ran to draped plush dresses—for
Art; to wreaths of silken flowerets in the hair—
for Femininity; and, somewhere between the
two adornments, to chain-drive the *pince-nez*—
for Astigmatism. The gentlemen were small
and somewhat in need of dusting.
—*Dorothy Parker*

221

What I don't like about office Christmas
parties is looking for a job the next day.

—*Phyllis Diller*

Pets and Animals

Some people say that cats are sneaky, evil,
and cruel. True, and they have many other
fine qualities as well.

—*Missy Dizick*

My husband and I are either going to buy a
dog or have a child. We can't decide whether
to ruin our carpet or ruin our lives.

—*Rita Rudner*

Did you ever walk into a room and forget why you walked in? I think that is how dogs spend their lives.

—*Sue Murphy*

Dogs come when they're called. Cats take a message and get back to you.

—*Mary Bly*

There are three basic personality factors in cats: The kind who run up when you say hello and rub against you in cheap romance; the kind who run away certain that you mean to ravish them; and the kind who just look back and don't move a muscle. I love all three kinds.

—*Eve Babitz*

223

When raising
rabbits, it
doesn't take
long to
double your
bunny back.

—Marcelene Cox

My parents ran a petting zoo and a heavy-petting zoo for the people who really like animals.

— *Ellen DeGeneres*

Long after the bomb falls and you and your good deeds are gone, cockroaches will still be here, prowling the streets like armored cars.

— *Tama Janowitz*

No animal should ever jump on the dining room furniture unless absolutely certain that he can hold his own in the conversation.

— *Fran Lebowitz*

I wonder if other dogs think poodles are members of a weird religious cult.

— *Rita Rudner*

FUNNY LADIES

A man who was loved by three hundred
women singled me out to live with him. Why?
I was the only one without a cat.
                                    —Elayne Boosler

I found out why cats drink out of the toilet.
My mother told me it's because the water is
cold in there. And I'm like, how did my
mother know that?
                                    —Wendy Liebman

Dogs act exactly the way we would act if we
had no shame.
                                    —Cynthia Heimel

The more I know about men the more I like dogs.
                                    —Gloria Allred

I just like bossing my dogs [not men or women] around. Because they listen.

—*Penny Marshall*

Don't accept your dog's admiration as con-clusive evidence that you are wonderful.

—*Ann Landers*

Dogs are the most amazing creatures; they give unconditional love. For me they are the role model for being alive.

—*Gilda Radner*

I had a dog named Dung for years, so I'm overcompensating.

—*Molly Ivins, on her dog named Athena*

Politics and Politicians

It's useless to hold a person to anything he says while he's in love, drunk, or running for office.

—Shirley MacLaine

When men in politics are together, testosterone poisoning makes them insane.

—Peggy Noonan

I've been married to one Marxist and one Fascist, and neither one would take the garbage out.

—Lee Grant

Why don't the feminists support Paula Jones
the way they supported Anita Hill? For the
same reason the blacks don't support Idi Amin
the way they supported Martin Luther King.
Why don't the Republicans support Timothy
McVeigh the way they support the NRA?

—*Elayne Boosler*

I will feel equality has arrived when we can
elect to office women who are as incompetent
as some of the men who are already there.

—*Maureen Reagan*

A leader who keeps his ear to the ground
allows his rear end to become a target.

—*Angie Papadakis*

And who knows? Somewhere out there in this audience may even be someone who will one day follow my footsteps, and preside over the White House as the president's spouse. I wish him well!

—Barbara Bush, in a commencement address at Wellesley College

Calling George Bush shallow is like calling a dwarf short.

—Molly Ivins

George Bush reminds every woman of her first husband.

—Jane O'Reilly

One of the things about equality is not just that
you be treated equally to a man, but that you
treat yourself equally to the way you treat a man.
— *Marlo Thomas*

The president of today is just the postage
stamp of tomorrow.

— *Gracie Allen*

Women arc being considered as candidates for
vice president of the United States because it is
the worst job in America. It's amazing that men
will take it. A job with real power is first lady.
I'd be willing to run for that. As far as the men
who are running for president are concerned,
they aren't even people I would date.

— *Nora Ephron*

The reason there are so few female politicians is that it is too much trouble to put makeup on two faces.

—*Maureen Murphy*

The position of first lady has no rules, just precedent, so its evolution has been at a virtual standstill for years. If Martha Washington didn't do it, then no one is sure it should be done.

—*Paula Poundstone*

Ninety-eight percent of the adults in this country are decent, hardworking, honest Americans. It's the other lousy 2 percent that get all the publicity. But then we elected them.

—*Lily Tomlin*

Relationships, Dating, and Singlehood

My grandmother's ninety. She's dating. He's ninety-three. It's great. They never argue. They can't hear each other.

— *Cathy Ladman*

All discarded lovers should be given a second chance, but with somebody else.

— *Mae West*

Constant togetherness is fine—but only for Siamese twins.

— *Victoria Billings*

Getting along with men isn't what's truly important. The vital knowledge is how to get along with one man.

— *Phyllis McGinley*

This guy says, "I'm perfect for you, 'cause I'm a cross between a macho man and a sensitive man." I said, "Oh, a gay trucker?"

— *Judy Tenuta*

I will not go out with a man who wears more jewelry than me, and I'll never, ever go to bed with a man who calls me Babe. Other than that, however, I'm real flexible.

— *Linda Sunshine*

Mr. Right is now a guy who hasn't been laid in fifteen years.

—*Elayne Boosler*

Younger men are more supportive and a lot less demanding, and they also have more time for their relationships.

—*Cher*

The most important thing in a relationship between a man and a woman is that one of them must be good at taking orders.

—*Linda Festa*

I went out to dinner with this man. . . . At least he was a gentleman: He carried my tray.

—*Jenny Jones*

235

I think, therefore I'm single.

— *Liz Winston*

Never judge someone by who he's in love with; judge him by his friends. People fall in love with the most appalling people. Take a cool, appraising glance at his pals.

— *Cynthia Heimel*

We had a lot in common: I loved him and he loved him.

— *Shelley Winters*

I've been on so many blind dates, I should get a free dog.

— *Wendy Liebman*

A woman without a man is like a fish without a bicycle.

—Gloria Steinem

FUNNY LADIES

I hate when I go to singles bars. Men will always come up to me and say, "Hey, cupcake, can I buy you a drink?" I always wanted to say, "No, but I'll take the three bucks."

— *Margaret Smith*

A good place to meet men is at the dry cleaner's. These men have jobs and usually bathe.

— *Rita Rudner*

I love being single. It's almost like being rich.

— *Sue Grafton*

I want a man in my life but not in my house. Just connect the VCR and get out.

— *Joy Behar*

Being in therapy is great. I spend an hour just talking about myself. It's kind of like being the guy on a date.

—*Caroline Rhea*

I don't need a man to rectify my existence. The most profound relationship we'll ever have is the one with ourselves.

—*Shirley MacLaine*

A woman needs a man like a fish needs a net.

—*Cynthia Heimel*

I went out with someone. Three years. The worst relationship. I'm talking one of those love-hate things. We both loved him and hated me.

—*Carol Siskind*

When you're single again, at the beginning you're very optimistic and you say, "I want to meet someone who's really smart, really sweet, really sensitive." And six months later you're like, "Lord, any mammal with a day job."

— *Carol Leifer*

It's like magic. When you live by yourself, all your annoying habits are gone!

— *Merrill Markoe*

A girl can wait for the right man to come along, but in the meantime, that still doesn't mean she can't have a wonderful time with all the wrong ones.

— *Cher*

I'm a firm believer in two things: I like men to be men and I like them to care about me and to take care of me. I'm willing to let them do that. If a man wants to be part of a lady's life, he needs to come on strong and come on caring and be prepared. The other part of that is beyond a man's or a woman's control. If something special is going to happen, it's a product of who that man is and who that woman is. If that chemistry is there, you don't have to do anything—just let it happen.

—*Shelley Long*

Whenever I date a guy, I think, Is this the man I want my children to spend their weekends with?

—*Rita Rudner*

Before I didn't [date] because I didn't want
to. Now I don't do it because (a) Denzel
Washington is married, and (b) I don't see
where you'd fit it in. Even without the baby,
I don't have any time. Besides, if you go to
bed with somebody, when do you have time
to read?

— *Paula Poundstone*

Hookers! How do they do it? How could any
woman sleep with a man without having a
dinner and a movie first?

— *Elayne Boosler*

She always believed in the old adage—leave
them while you're looking good.

— *Anita Loos*

What ever happened to the kind of love
leech that lived in his car and dropped by
once a month to throw up and use you for
your shower? Now all these pigs want is a
commitment.

—Judy Tenuta

Being an old maid is like death by drowning,
a really delightful sensation after you cease
to struggle.

—Edna Ferber

For a single woman, preparing for company
means wiping the lipstick off the milk carton.

—Elayne Boosler

I go to singles bars. And you always tell strangers your life history. It becomes such a rap. I have mine down to a science. I repeat myself like a stewardess. "Good evening. My name is Carol Roberts, I'm four foot, eleven and one-half. And I've been cruising you at an altitude of sea level for just over an hour and a half. I'm a Gemini, Sagittarius rising, New York born and bred. In the event we should have a one-night stand, my blouse will automatically pop open and two breasts will emerge." And so on.

—*Carol Roberts*

I want a man who's kind and understanding. Is that too much to ask of a millionaire?

—*Zsa Zsa Gabor*

Sex

Dr. Ruth says that, as women, we should tell our lovers how to make love to us. My boyfriend goes nuts if I tell him how to drive.

—*Pam Stone*

I don't know what I am, dahling. I've tried several varieties of sex. The conventional position makes me claustrophobic. And the others give me a stiff neck or lockjaw.

—*Tallulah Bankhead*

I always wanted to be Emily Dickinson because no one ever wrote on the side of *her* garage: "Emily puts out."

—*Margaret Smith*

I married a German. Every night I dress up as Poland and he invades me.

— *Bette Midler*

I have never quite understood this sex symbol business, but if I'm going to be a symbol of something, I'd rather have it be sex than some of the other things they've got symbols for.

— *Marilyn Monroe*

I like my furniture too much.

— *Margaret Cho, on her distaste for sex*

Sex is the most fun you can have without smiling.

— *Madonna*

[My closet] was huge, had a foyer, a turnstile, a few locks, dead bolts, a burglar alarm with code that all had to be deactivated, decoded before [I] could ever go for the door handle.
— *Kate Clinton, on coming out of the closet*

What does "good in bed" mean to me? When I'm sick and I stay home from school propped up with lots of pillows watching TV and my mom brings me soup—that's good in bed.
— *Brooke Shields*

Sex is hardly ever just about sex.
— *Shirley MacLaine*

Well, I love to travel, so far be it for me to judge anyone's traveling choices. Live in the moment. That allows you to make a decision based on how you feel. Having a passport doesn't hurt either.

*—Shelley Long, on women who go
all the way on the first date*

Never refer to your wedding night as the "original amateur hour."

—Phyllis Diller

My husband complained to me. He said, "I can't remember when we last had sex," and I said, "Well I can and that's why we ain't doing it."

—Roseanne

To me the term "sexual freedom" meant freedom from having to have sex.
>   —*Jane Wagner*

After sex, the man dies.
>   —*Emily Levine, on her sexual fantasies*

A young man who grows up expecting to dominate sexually is bound to be somewhat startled by a young woman who wants sex as much as he does, and multiorgasmic sex at that.
>   —*Nora Ephron*

After we made love he took a piece of chalk and made an outline of my body.
>   —*Joan Rivers*

249

Remember when safe sex meant doing it
when your parents were out of town?
—*Reno (Karen Renaud)*

Sex is a pleasurable exercise in plumbing,
but be careful or you'll get yeast in your
drain tap.
—*Rita Mae Brown*

Girls who put out are tramps. Girls who don't
are ladies. This is, however, a rather archaic use
of the word. Should one of you boys happen
upon a girl who doesn't put out, do not jump
to the conclusion that you have found a lady.
What you have probably found is a lesbian.
—*Fran Lebowitz*

*Anyone who's
a great kisser
I'm always
interested in.*

—Cher

The more sex becomes a nonissue in people's
lives, the happier they are.

—Shirley MacLaine

Kissing a feller with a beard is like a picnic.
You don't mind going through a little brush
to get there.

—Minnie Pearl

Boredom is often the cause of promiscuity,
and always its result.

—Mignon McLaughlin

If sex is such a natural phenomenon, how
come there are so many books on how to?

—Bette Midler

Nothing is either all masculine or all feminine except having sex.

— *Marlo Thomas*

The act of sex . . . is man's last desperate stand at superintendency.

— *Bette Davis*

Too much of a good thing can be taxing.

— *Mae West*

In my sex fantasy, nobody ever loves me for my mind.

— *Nora Ephron*

If sex isn't a joke, what is it?

— Nella Larsen

Whatever else can be said about sex, it cannot be called a dignified performance.

— Helen Lawrenson

When you look back at your life . . . what you really find out is that the only person you really go to bed with is yourself.

— Shirley MacLaine

The zipless fuck is the purest thing there is. And it is rarer than a unicorn. And I have never had one.

— Erica Jong

Sex is God's joke on human beings.

—*Bette Davis*

You can imagine how shocked Miss Manners was to hear where babies come from. Babies, it seems, no longer appear from vegetable gardens or express deliveries by large birds (who refuse to leave them if you're not home to sign for them, even though they never tell you exactly when they will arrive).

—*Judith Martin, Miss Manners*

What *isn't* funny about sex?

—*Roz Warren*

It's been so long since I made love I can't even remember who gets tied up.

—*Joan Rivers*

I used to be a virgin, but I gave it up because there was no money in it.

—*Marsha Warfield*

Personally I know nothing about sex because I've always been married.

—*Zsa Zsa Gabor*

Sex when you're married is like going to a 7-Eleven. There's not much variety, but at three in the morning it's always there.

—*Carol Leifer*

The difference between pornography and erotica is lighting.

—*Gloria Leonard*

Women complain about sex more often than men. Their gripes fall into two major categories: (1) Not enough. (2) Too much.

—*Ann Landers*

If all these sweet young things were laid end to end, I wouldn't be the slightest bit surprised.

—*Dorothy Parker*

If men knew what women laughed about, they would never sleep with us.

—*Erica Jong*

Hickeys are like PG-13 movies. You think
they're pretty hot stuff after being limited to
G and PG, but you never bother with them
once you're seriously into R.

—Judy Markey

Don't bother discussing sex with small
children. They rarely have anything
to add.

—Fran Lebowitz

My lesbianism is an act of Christian charity.
All those women out there are praying for
a man, and I'm giving them my share.

—Rita Mae Brown

Sexual Attraction and Sexuality

I go for two kinds of men. The kind with muscles, and the kind without.

—Mae West

Sex appeal is 50 percent what you've got and 50 percent what people think you've got.

—Sophia Loren

Sick and perverted always appeals to me.

—Madonna

I hate the term "in the closet." Until recently I hated the word *lesbian*, too. I've said it enough now that it doesn't bother me. But *lesbian* sounded like somebody with some kind of disease. I didn't like that, so I used the word *gay* more often.

— Ellen DeGeneres

If homosexuality is a disease, let's all call in queer to work. "Hello, can't work today. Still queer."

— Robin Taylor

Men aren't attracted to me by my mind. They're attracted by what I don't mind.

— Gypsy Rose Lee

You can seduce a man without taking anything off, without even touching him.

— *Rae Dawn Chong*

I have no-fail chemistry. A guy turns me on, he's the wrong one for me.

— *Linda Barnes*

To attract men, I wear a perfume called New Car Interior.

— *Rita Rudner*

I feel like a million tonight—but one at a time.

— *Mae West*

If somebody
makes me
laugh, I'm
his slave
for life.

—Bette Midler

The only men who are too young are
the ones who write their love letters in
crayon, wear pajamas with feet, or fly for
half fare.

— *Phyllis Diller*

A sex symbol becomes a thing. I hate being
a thing.

— *Marilyn Monroe*

The requirements of romantic love are
difficult to satisfy in the trunk of a
Dodge Dart.

— *Lisa Alther*

I don't care what X or Y does. I didn't do it to make a political statement. I did it selfishly for myself and because I thought it was a great thing for the show, which desperately needed a point of view. If other people come out, that's fine. I mean, it would be great if for no other reason than just to show the diversity, so it's not just the extremes. Because unfortunately those are the people who get the most attention on the news. . . . The whole point of what I'm doing is acceptance of everyone's differences. It's just that I don't want them representing the entire gay community, and I'm sure they don't want me representing them. We're individuals.

—*Ellen DeGeneres, on revealing she is gay*

Shopping

Let's face it: Bo might know baseball, but
he doesn't know a thing about visible panty
lines. If sporting goods companies want our
dollars, they've got to start speaking our
language.

— *Susanna Levin*

Do you shop at Bloomingdale's? Do you like
that store? I hate that [expletive] store. I
always feel shorter and fatter in that store. . . .
I have to go over to Alexander's to regain
my height.

— *Joy Behar*

265

One quarter of what you buy will turn out to
be mistakes.

—Delia Ephron

Shopping is better than sex. If you're not
satisfied after shopping you can make an
exchange for something you really like.

—Adrienne Gusoff

If men liked shopping, they'd call it research.

—Cynthia Nelms

I found out it's fun to go shopping. It's such a
feminine thing to do.

—Marilyn Monroe

Know the difference between Giant and
Jumbo? Between two ounce and a *big* two
ounce? Between a quart and a *full* quart?
What's a *tall* twenty-four-inch? What does
extra long mean? Who's kidding who?
—*Marya Mannes*

Sports and Athletes

If it weren't for baseball, many kids wouldn't
know what a millionaire looked like.
—*Phyllis Diller*

If a man watches three football games in a
row, he should be declared legally dead.
—*Erma Bombeck*

Give a man a fish and he has food for a day; teach him how to fish and you can get rid of him for the entire weekend.

—*Zenna Schaffer*

I ask people why they have deer heads on their walls, and they say, "Because it's such a beautiful animal." There you go. Well, I think my mother's attractive, but I have *photographs* of her.

—*Ellen DeGeneres*

I do not participate in any sport with ambulances at the bottom of a hill.

—*Erma Bombeck*

If it wasn't
for golf,
I'd probably
be the fat
lady in the
circus now.

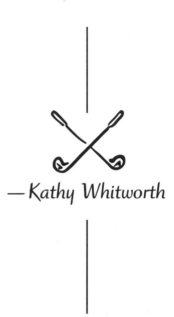

—Kathy Whitworth

Men are very confident people. My husband is so confident that when he watches sports on television, he thinks that if he concentrates he can help his team. If the team is in trouble, he coaches the players from our living room, and if they're really in trouble, I have to get off the phone in case they call him.

—*Rita Rudner*

When I want to really blast one, I just loosen my girdle and let 'er fly.

—*Babe Didrikson Zaharias*

The one nice thing about sports is that they prove men do have emotions and are not afraid to show them.

—*Jane O'Reilly*

Generally speaking, I look upon [sports] as dangerous and tiring activities performed by people with whom I share nothing except the right to trial by jury.

—*Fran Lebowitz*

Success and Failure

Success to me is having ten honeydew melons and only eating the top half of each slice.

—*Barbra Streisand*

Success is a two-bladed golden sword; it knights one and stabs one at the same time.

—*Mae West*

The worst part of success is to try to find someone who is happy for you.

—*Bette Midler*

I succeeded by saying what everyone else is thinking.

—*Joan Rivers*

It's a little depressing to become number one because the only place you can go from there is down.

—*Doris Day*

If at first you don't succeed, why go on and make a fool of yourself?

—*Susanna Pomeory*

I'll match my flops with anybody's but I wouldn't have missed 'em. Flops are a part of life's menu and I've never been a girl to miss out on any of the courses.

— Rosalind Russell

I climbed the ladder of success wrong by wrong.

— Patricia Brooks

Nothing fails like success; nothing is so defeated as yesterday's triumphant Cause.

— Phyllis McGinley

Sometimes I worry about being a success in a mediocre world.

— Lily Tomlin

Nothing succeeds like address.

—*Fran Lebowitz*

When you're successful, the thing that attracts men to you as a date is exactly what drives them away as a mate.

—*Carrie Fisher*

Success is a great deodorant.

—*Elizabeth Taylor*

There is no point at which you can say, "Well, I'm successful now. I might as well take a nap."

—*Carrie Fisher*

Technology and Progress

A car is just a moving, giant handbag! You never have actually to carry groceries, or dry cleaning, or anything! You can have five pairs of shoes with you at all times!

—Cynthia Heimel

The wheel is nice. But I cannot picture functioning without an answering machine. Let's face it, someone was eventually going to come up with the wheel. The answering machine took real innovation.

—Paula Poundstone, when asked what's mankind's greatest invention

On a plane you can pick up more and better people than on any other public conveyance since the stagecoach.

—Anita Loos

Whoever said progress was a positive thing has never been to Florida or California.

—Rita Mae Brown

What a lot we lost when we stopped writing letters. You can't reread a phone call.

—Liz Carpenter

What do people mean when they say the computer went down on me?

—Marilyn Pittman

The pilot says, "We are currently hurtling through the air at five hundred miles per hour. Please feel free to move about the cabin." Then you land. You're rolling to the gate at one mile per hour and you hear: "You must remain seated for your own safety! Sit down!" I'm wondering, could we take off again? I need my coat from the overhead.

—*Carol Leifer*

State-of-the-art automation will never beat the wastebasket when it comes to speeding up efficiency in the office.

—*Ann Landers*

You heard about this feller fresh from the farm and he goes into a big department store and he gets on the escalator for the first time in his life. And there he is trying to go up on a down escalator. I hollered at him to get off and he hollers back, "Leave me alone, gal! Cain't you see I'm a-gainin' on it!"

— *Minnie Pearl*

I don't like driving very much. That makes me very unhappy, because I scream a lot in the car, but other than that, life is actually pretty good.

— *Whoopi Goldberg*

I feel about airplanes the way I feel about diets. It seems to me that they are wonderful things for other people to go on.

—*Erma Bombeck*

The Internet is one of those things I'm not sure about. I just don't get it. And technology is moving at such a rate that I can't really keep up with it. I was in London recently, reading about these chips they want to put into little children. I'm not sure. I don't trust bar codes. Why can't I read them? Why can't I know what that bar code says? It's a secret code and we're kept out of the loop. Scary.

—*Whoopi Goldberg*

They say [computers] make paying your bills so much easier. How hard was it before? Were they still stacking coins in a counting house, wearing those gloves with no fingertips?

—*Paula Poundstone*

Vices

Instant gratification is not soon enough.

—*Meryl Streep*

I don't like pot anymore—I forgot why.

—*Margaret Cho*

Many are saved from sin by being so inept at it.

—*Mignon McLaughlin*

*One more
drink and
I'll be under
the host.*

—Dorothy Parker

Sin has always been an ugly word, but it has been made so in a new sense over the last half century. It has been made not only ugly but passé. People are no longer sinful, they are only immature or underprivileged or frightened or, more particularly, sick.

— *Phyllis McGinley*

I used to be Snow White, but I drifted.

— *Mae West*

It's the good girls who keep the diaries; the bad girls never have the time.

— *Tallulah Bankhead*

People always come up to me and say that my smoking is bothering them. . . . Well, it's killing me.

—*Wendy Liebman*

Instant gratification takes too long.

—*Carrie Fisher*

Now the only thing I miss about sex is the cigarette afterward. Next to the first one in the morning, it's the best one of all. It tasted so good that even if I had been frigid I would have pretended otherwise just to be able to smoke it.

—*Florence King*

The problem with people who have no vices is that generally you can be pretty sure they're going to have some pretty annoying virtues.
— *Elizabeth Taylor*

There ain't no joy in a high—none. You *think* there's a joy in a high because it feels good temporarily. But it feels good less and less often, so you've got to do it more and more often. It ain't your friend.
— *Whoopi Goldberg*

Uncle Nabob takes a drink every now and then to steady his nerves. He gets pretty steady. Sometimes he don't move at all.
— *Minnie Pearl*

One of my favorite [antidrug campaigns] was
Nancy Reagan going through a crack house
and afterwards saying that a crack house is
a terrible place. But you had the feeling for
her it had something to do with the plaid
couch. . . . It was a decorating thing.

— *Kate Clinton*

The wages of sin are death, but after taxes are
taken out, it's just a tired feeling.

— *Paula Poundstone*

How many people remember when the worst
thing about crack was if you stepped on it you
broke your mother's back?

— *Carol Leifer*

Smoking . . . is downright dangerous. Most people who smoke will eventually contract a fatal disease and die. But they don't brag about it, do they? Most people who ski, play professional football, or drive race cars will not die—at least not in the act—and yet they are the ones with the glamorous images, the expensive equipment, and the mythic proportions. Why this should be I cannot say, unless it is simply that the average American does not know a daredevil when he sees one.

— *Fran Lebowitz*

When women go wrong, men go right with them.

— *Mae West*

Lead me not into temptation; I can find the way myself.

—*Rita Mae Brown*

Never practice two vices at once.

—*Tallulah Bankhead*

I always wanted to blunt and blur what was painful. My idea [in taking drugs] was pain reduction and mind expansion, but I ended up with mind reduction and pain expansion.

—*Carrie Fisher*

Food, sex, and liquor create their own appetite.

—*Sheilah Graham*

When the sun comes up, I have morals again.
— *Elayne Boosler*

Alcoholism isn't a spectator sport. Eventually the whole family gets to play.
— *Joyce Rebeta-Burditt*

Liquor is such a nice substitute for facing adult life.
— *Dorothy B. Hughes*

Good girls go to heaven, bad girls go everywhere.
— *Helen Gurley Brown*

Having a wonderful time. Wish I were here.
>— *Carrie Fisher*

Cocaine habit forming? Of course not, I ought to know. I've been using it for years.
>— *Tallulah Bankhead*

Smoking is, if not my life, then at least my hobby. I love to smoke. Smoking is fun. Smoking is cool. Smoking is, as far as I am concerned, the entire point of being an adult.
>— *Fran Lebowitz*

Even though a number of people have tried, no one has yet found a way to drink for a living.
>— *Jean Kerr*

I used to smoke two packs a day and I just hate being a nonsmoker. . . . But I will never consider myself a nonsmoker. Because I always find smokers the most interesting people at the table.

—*Michelle Pfeiffer*

Wealth and Poverty

I've been rich and I've been poor; rich is better.
—*Sophie Tucker*

Money is of value for what it buys, and in love it buys time, place, intimacy, comfort, and a private corner alone.

—*Mae West*

Wouldn't you think some sociologist would have done a comparative study by now to prove, as I have always suspected, that there is a higher proportion of undeserving rich than poor?

—*Molly Ivins*

Poverty makes you funny.

—*Kim Wayans*

Whether he admits it or not, a man has been brought up to look at money as a sign of his virility, a symbol of his power, a bigger phallic symbol than a Porsche.

—*Victoria Billings*

I'm having trouble managing the mansion. What I need is a wife.

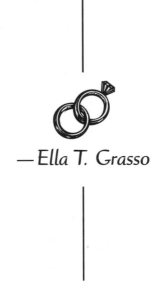

—Ella T. Grasso

I like men who are prematurely wealthy.
—*Joan Rivers*

The two most beautiful words in the English language are "check enclosed."
—*Dorothy Parker*

You hear a lot of dialogue on the death of the American family. Families aren't dying. They're merging into big conglomerates.
—*Erma Bombeck*

I do want to get rich, but I never want to do what there is to do to get rich.
—*Gertrude Stein*

We've had trickle-down economics for the country for ten years now, and most of us aren't even damp yet.

—Molly Ivins

It's like, the clothes are in jail. I go in every so often and say, "Could I just see the pants?"

—Paula Poundstone, on being broke and unable to reclaim her clothes from the dry cleaner's

I was once so poor I didn't know where my next husband was coming from.

—Mae West

A diamond is the only kind of ice that keeps a girl warm.

—Elizabeth Taylor

Money is always there, but the pockets change.
—*Gertrude Stein*

Some people get so rich they lose all respect
for humanity. That's how rich I want to be.
—*Rita Rudner*

I don't want to make money. I just want to be
wonderful.
—*Marilyn Monroe*

You don't seem to realize that a poor person
who is unhappy is in a better position than
a rich person who is unhappy. Because the
poor person has hope. He thinks money
would help.

—*Jean Kerr*

How often the rich like to play at being poor.
A rather nasty game, I've always thought.

—Lillian Hellman

Wisecracks and Witticisms

Honey, get off the cross. Somebody else needs
the wood.

—Dolly Parton

If you can't say something good about
someone, sit right here by me.

*—Alice Roosevelt Longworth, a phrase
she embroidered on a pillow*

Her only flair is in her nostrils.

—Pauline Kael

If you want to say it with flowers, a single rose says: "I'm cheap!"

—*Delta Burke*

Have you ever been in therapy? No? You should try it. It's like a really easy game show where the correct answer to every question is: "Because of my mother."

—*Robin Greenspan*

The meaning of the title is pornographic, but I'm using it metaphorically.

—*Carrie Fisher*

If brains were money, you'd need to take out a loan to buy a cup of coffee.

—*Shelley Long*

If the universe is a high school, then our culture is definitely eighth grade. It's run by eighth-grade boys, and the way these boys show a girl they like her is by humiliating her and making her cry.

—*Merrill Markoe*

Is she fat? Her favorite food is seconds.

—*Joan Rivers*

I've been on a calendar, but never on time.

—*Marilyn Monroe*

She's the original good time that was had by all.

—*Bette Davis*

I like two kinds of men: domestic and imported.

—*Mae West*

Women on Men

It is funny. The two things men are most proud of are the things that any man can do, and does in the same way—being drunk and being the father of their son.

—*Gertrude Stein*

You can always tell when someone's lying to you, because they're male.

—*Caroline Rhea*

Men are completely nuts.

—*Merrill Markoe*

They're all different, like snowflakes.

—*Margaret Cho, on male sex organs*

The male ego with few exceptions is elephan-
tine to start with.

—Bette Davis

My ancestors wandered lost in the wilderness
for forty years because even in biblical times,
men would not stop to ask for directions.

—Elayne Boosler

If this were a logical world, men would ride
sidesaddle.

—Rita Mae Brown

If you never want to see a man again, say,
"I love you. I want to marry you. I want to
have children"; they leave skid marks.

—Rita Rudner

I like my pigs as brief as possible.
> —*Judy Tenuta, when asked whether*
> *she preferred boxers or briefs*

Men are always ready to respect anything that bores them.
> —*Marilyn Monroe*

A male gynecologist is like an auto mechanic who has never owned a car.
> —*Carrie Snow*

We got new evidence as to what motivated man to walk upright: to free his hands for masturbation.
> —*Jane Wagner*

The only place men want depth in a woman is her décolletage.

—Zsa Zsa Gabor

A guy is a lump like a doughnut. So, first you gotta get rid of all the stuff his mom did to him. And then you gotta get rid of all that macho crap that they pick up from beer commercials. And then there's my personal favorite, the male ego.

—Roseanne

From the viewpoint of many men, there are two stages in a woman's life: prey and invisible. After a certain age, when they don't want to fuck you anymore, they don't see you at all.

—Cynthia Heimel

The men are too busy running the world into the ground. And men still haven't gotten over the reality that it's women who have the children and that they can only produce bodily fluids.

—*Reno (Karen Renaud)*

The fastest way to a man's heart is through his chest.

—*Roseanne*

If it's true that men are such beasts—this must account for the fact that most women are animal lovers.

—*Farrah Fawcett*

Time wounds all heels.

—*Jane Sherwood Ace*

Beware of men on airplanes. The minute a
man reaches thirty thousand feet, he immediately becomes consumed by distasteful sexual
fantasies that involve doing uncomfortable
things in those tiny toilets. These men should
not be encouraged, their fantasies are sadly
low-rent and unimaginative. Affect an aloof,
cool demeanor as soon as any man tries to
draw you out. Unless, of course, he's the pilot.

—*Cynthia Heimel*

A woman has got to love a bad man once or
twice in her life to be thankful for a good one.

—*Mae West*

There are men I could spend eternity with,
but not this life.

—*Kathleen Norris*

I like a man who wears a wedding ring. 'Cause without it, they're like a shark without a fin. You pretty much gotta know they're out there.
— *Brett Butler*

All men are not slimy warthogs. Some men are silly giraffes, some woebegone puppies, some insecure frogs. But if one is not careful, those slimy warthogs can ruin it for all the others.
— *Cynthia Heimel*

Summer bachelors, like summer breezes, are never as cool as they pretend to be.
— *Nora Ephron*

Macho does not prove mucho.
— *Zsa Zsa Gabor*

I've been asked to say a couple of words about my husband, Fang. How about *short* and *cheap*?

— *Phyllis Diller*

Beware of men who cry. It's true that men who cry are sensitive to and in touch with feelings, but the only feelings they tend to be sensitive to and in touch with are their own.

— *Nora Ephron*

When he is late for dinner and I know he must be either having an affair or lying dead in the street, I always hope he's dead.

— *Judith Viorst*

A strong man doesn't have to be dominant toward a woman. He doesn't match his strength against a woman weak with love for him. He matches it against the world.

—*Marilyn Monroe*

My biting sarcasm and shrill hysteria can make mincemeat of any man who looks as if he's about to trifle with my feelings, abandon me like my daddy did, or break my heart.

—*LaDonna Mason*

There are plenty of men who philander during the summer, to be sure, but they are usually the same lot who philander during the winter—albeit with less convenience.

—*Nora Ephron*

307

If a man is talking in the forest, and there is no woman there to hear him, is he still wrong?

—Jenny Weber

The best way to get husbands to do something is to suggest that perhaps they are too old to do it.

—*Shirley MacLaine*

I require only three things in a man: He must be handsome, ruthless, and stupid.

—*Dorothy Parker*

Women on Women

When a man gives his opinion he's a man.
When a woman gives her opinion she's a bitch.

—*Bette Davis*

Women's virtue is man's greatest invention.

—*Cornelia Otis Skinner*

FUNNY LADIES

Women want men, careers, money, children,
friends, luxury, comfort, independence, freedom, respect, love, and a three-dollar panty
hose that won't run.

— *Phyllis Diller*

Women of today . . . You know the kind: "Hi!
I just had a baby an hour ago, and I'm back
at work already. And while I was delivering,
I took a seminar on tax-shelter options."

— *Carol Leifer*

A woman's a woman until the day she dies,
but a man's a man only as long as he can.

— *Jackie "Moms" Mabley*

A man has to be Joe McCarthy to be called ruthless. All a woman has to do is put you on hold.

—*Marlo Thomas*

The thing women have got to learn is that nobody gives you power. You just take it.

—*Roseanne*

If women ruled the world and we all got massages, there would be no war.

—*Carrie Snow*

Unfortunately, sometimes people don't hear you until you scream.

—*Stefanie Powers*

God gave women intuition and femininity.
Used properly, the combination easily jumbles
the brain of any man I've ever met.
—Farrah Fawcett

We should try to bring to any power what we
have as women. We will destroy it all if we try
to imitate that absolutely unfeeling, driving
ambition that we have seen coming at us
across the desk.
—Colleen Dewhurst

Were women meant to do everything—work
and have babies?
—Candice Bergen

Women complain about premenstrual syndrome, but I think of it as the only time of the month I can be myself.

— *Roseanne*

Being a woman is of special interest only to aspiring male transsexuals. To actual women it is merely a good excuse not to play football.

— *Fran Lebowitz*

I'm just a person trapped inside a woman's body.

— *Elayne Boosler*

Women on Themselves

Take me or leave me; or, as is the usual order of things, both.

— *Dorothy Parker*

I was never unfeminine, but I came with a package of children and a husband. If you don't have that, you would have to be extremely careful not to appear butch, or too negative. They're not going to buy negative.

— *Phyllis Diller*

I was street-smart—but unfortunately the street was Rodeo Drive.

— *Carrie Fisher*

I guess I just prefer to see the dark side of things. The glass is always half empty. And cracked. And I just cut my lip on it. And chipped a tooth.

—*Janeane Garofalo*

I know I've got a big mouth. I guess I've won a lot of fans by stretching it to make it look even bigger than it is. That's swell and I'm grateful. You're lucky in this business if people like you for any reason.

—*Martha Raye*

I don't consider myself a female comedian. My gender has nothing to do with my profession. I don't talk about life as a woman.

—*Ellen DeGeneres*

I am the modern, intelligent, independent-type woman. In other words, a girl who cannot get a man.

—*Shelley Winters*

[*Sesame Street*] told me I was too funny to write for them, and I burst into tears. I'm someone who's always tried to be normal—it's just never worked out.

—*Wendy Wasserstein*

What Asian role models were there when I grew up? There was that lady who said, "Ancient Chinese Secret, huh?" And there was that show *Kung Fu*. But they should have called it "That Guy's Not Really Chinese."

—*Margaret Cho*

I sometimes think I was born to live up to my name. How could I be anything else but what I am having been named Madonna? I would either have ended up a nun or this.

—*Madonna*

I'm an experienced woman; I've been around. . . . Well, all right, I might not've been around, but I've been . . . nearby.

—*Mary Tyler Moore*

Oh, I'm so inadequate—and I love myself!

—*Meg Ryan*

Ducking for apples—change one letter and it's the story of my life.

—*Dorothy Parker*

I have six locks on my door all in a row. When I go out, I lock every other one. I figure no matter how long somebody stands there picking the locks, they are always locking three.

—*Elayne Boosler*

I tried to charm the pants off Bob Dylan, but everyone will be disappointed to learn that I was unsuccessful. I got close—a couple of fast feels in the front seat of a Cadillac.

—*Bette Midler*

I'm just a loudmouthed middle-aged colored lady . . . and a lot of people think I'm crazy. Maybe you do too, but I never stop to wonder why I'm not like other people. The mystery to me is why more people aren't like me.

—*Florynce Kennedy*

I have the perfect face for radio.

—*Virginia Graham*

I'm not a cookie-baking mother. Well, that's not true. I am a cookie-baking mother. I'm exactly a cookie-baking mother, but I'm not a traditional cookie-baking mother.

—*Cher*

I would be Batman. I enjoy the costume—it comes with the plastic muscles so you instantly get a nice body—and you get to save people in trouble. Anonymously.

—*Rosie O'Donnell, when asked if she could be a man for a day who would she be and why*

319

I'm tough, ambitious, and I know exactly what
I want. If that makes me a bitch, okay.

—Madonna

I am a spy in the house of me. I report back
from the front lines of the battle that is me.
I am somewhat nonplussed by the event that
is my life.

—Carrie Fisher

I can hold a note as long as the Chase
Manhattan Bank.

—Ethel Merman

I'm certainly not a glamour girl. I don't think
I intimidate anyone.

—Valerie Harper

Please don't think me negligent or rude. I am
both, in effect, of course, but please don't
think me either.

— *Edna St. Vincent Millay*

[Elvis] appeared to me and told me I had to
start my own religion—that's Judyism, of
course—and I had to go forth and abuse
people with my accordion.

— *Judy Tenuta*

How can I believably be a dumb blonde? I'm
the furthest thing from it. I am intelligent. I
don't mean I have a great IQ. I just mean there's
always an intelligence present in what I do.

— *Madeline Kahn*

There are two reasons why I'm in show business, and I'm standing on both of them.
                                        —*Betty Grable*

Sometimes I want to clean up my desk and go out and say, Respect me, I'm a respectable grown-up, and other times I just want to jump into a paper bag and shake and bake myself to death.

                                        —*Wendy Wasserstein*

I don't want to smoke cigars or go to stag parties, wear Jockey shorts or pick up the check.
                                        —*Shelley Winters, on her antifeminism*

I believe in practicing prudence at least once every two or three years.

                                        —*Molly Ivins*

I never liked the men I loved, and I never loved the men I liked.

—*Fanny Brice*

I was raised to sense what someone wanted me to be and be that kind of person. It took me a long time not to judge myself through someone else's eyes.

—*Sally Field*

[I don't fit] into that perfect—and boring— Barbie doll image we have of women. I am what would result from Lucille Ball and Dick Van Dyke because I have red hair and trip over ottomans.

—*Mary Ellen Hooper*

The only parts left of my original body are
my elbows.

—*Phyllis Diller*

I have three phobias which, could I mute
them, would make my life as slick as a sonnet,
but as dull as ditch water: I hate to go to bed,
I hate to get up, and I hate to be alone.

—*Tallulah Bankhead*

Don't call me a saint. I don't want to be
dismissed that easily.

—*Dorothy Day*

I wouldn't say I invented tacky, but I definitely
brought it to its present high popularity.

—*Bette Midler*

I never go out unless I look like Joan Crawford the movie star. If you want to see the girl next door, go next door.

—Joan Crawford

I was thought to be stuck-up. I wasn't. I was just sure of myself. This is and always has been an unforgivable quality to the unsure.

—Bette Davis

Whatever you have read I have said is almost certainly untrue, except if it is funny, in which case I definitely said it.

—Tallulah Bankhead

Success didn't spoil me; I've always been insufferable.

—Fran Lebowitz

I was too old for a paper route, too young for
Social Security, and too tired for an affair.
> —*Erma Bombeck, on beginning her humor column*

I don't deserve any credit for turning the other
cheek as my tongue is always in it.
> —*Flannery O'Connor*

Well, [the accordion is] a special instrument
of love and submission. Actually, it's really
just a device to abuse all my followers. The
accordion is there to punish the pigs the way
they want to be punished. In fact, if you
want a man, the best thing to do is play the
squeeze-box on his head until he promises
to buy you a Porsche.
> —*Judy Tenuta*

After my screen test, the director clapped his hands gleefully and yelled, "She can't talk! She can't act! She's sensational!"

—*Ava Gardner*

I can ruin my reputation in five minutes; I don't need help.

—*Martha Graham*

Deep down, I'm pretty superficial.

—*Ava Gardner*

Whenever I have to choose between two evils, I always like to try the one I haven't tried before.

—*Mae West*

FUNNY LADIES

I have flabby thighs, but fortunately my stomach covers them.

—*Joan Rivers*

I have bursts of being a lady, but it doesn't last long.

—*Shelley Winters*

I don't remember anybody's name. How do you think the "dahling" thing got started?

—*Zsa Zsa Gabor*

Whenever I dwell for any length of time on my own shortcomings, they gradually begin to seem mild, harmless, rather engaging little things, not at all like the staring defects in other people's characters.

—*Margaret Halsey*

I never loved another person the way I loved myself.

—*Mae West*

I'm as pure as the driven slush.
—*Tallulah Bankhead*

Work and Careers

Adults are always asking little kids what they want to be when they grow up—'cause they're looking for ideas.

—*Paula Poundstone*

The trouble with the rat race is that even if you win, you're still a rat.

—*Lily Tomlin*

A genius is one who can do anything except
make a living.

—Joey Lauren Adams

There is no pleasure in having nothing to do;
the fun is in having lots to do and not doing it.

—Mary Wilson Little

Always be smarter than the people who
hire you.

—Lena Horne

I believe you are your work. Don't trade the
stuff of your life, time, for nothing more than
dollars. That's a rotten bargain.

—Rita Mae Brown

I don't know anything about luck. I've never banked on it, and I'm afraid of people who do. Luck to me is something else: hard work and realizing what is opportunity and what isn't.
— *Lucille Ball*

I decided to do something a little less emotionally damaging than being married.
— *Marsha Warfield on starting her stand-up career*

All jobs should be open to everybody, unless they actually require a penis or vagina.
— *Florynce Kennedy*

What do hookers do on their nights off, type?
— *Elayne Boosler*

331

I have a brain and a uterus and I use
them both.
> —Patricia Schroeder, on being asked how she could
> be both a congresswoman and a mother

Writing and Writers

Writers will happen in the best of families.
> —Rita Mae Brown

Writing is the only thing that, when I do it,
I don't feel I should be doing something else.
> —Gloria Steinem

I hope that one or two immortal lyrics will
come out of all this tumbling around.
> —Louise Bogan

Humorists can never start to take them- selves seriously. It's literary suicide.

—Erma Bombeck

Everywhere I go I'm asked if the universities stifle writers. My opinion is that they don't stifle enough of them. There's many a best-seller that could have been prevented by a good teacher.

— *Flannery O'Connor*

Writers have two main problems. One is writer's block, when the words won't come at all, and the other is logorrhea, when the words come so fast that they can hardly get into the waste-basket on time.

— *Cecilia Bartholomew*

References

Brain Candy http://members.aol.com/WordPlays/
words.html

The Quotations Archive www.aphids.com

Quotation Search www.starlingtech.com

Creative Quotations www.bemorecreative.com

She Said http://webpages.ainet.com/gosner/
quotationsarch/women.htm

Thought for Today
1996 http://webpages.ainet.com/gosner/
quotationsarch/tft96.htm

1995 http://webpages.ainet.com/gosner/
quotationsarch/tft95.htm

Stand-Up Comedians www.geocities.com/
CollegePark/Quad/5442/Stand-Up.htm

Paul Tomko's Collection of Humourous Quotes
www.tomkonic.com/quotes.htm

The Quotations Home Page
www.geocities.com/~spanoudi/quote-16.html

www.geocities.com/CapeCanaveral/5958/quote.html

www.geocities.com/SoHo/Coffeehouse/13114/
content.html

Adler, Gloria. *She Said, She Said: Strong Words from Strong-Minded Women.* New York: Avon Books, 1995.

Andrews, Robert. *Cassell Dictionary of Contemporary Quotations.* London: Cassell, 1996.

Augrade, Tony. *The Oxford Dictionary of Modern Quotations.* Oxford: Oxford University Press, 1991.

Beilenson, Evelyn L., and Ann Tenenbaum. *Wit and Wisdom of Famous American Women.* White Plains, N.Y.: Peter Pauper Press, 1986.

Biggs, Mary. *Women's Words: The Columbia Book of Quotations by Women.* New York: Columbia University Press, 1996.

Byrne, Robert. *1,911 Best Things Anybody Ever Said.* New York: Fawcett Books, 1988.

Conny, Beth Mende. *Winning Women: Quotations on Sports, Health and Fitness.* White Plains, N.Y.: Peter Pauper Press, 1993.

Edmonson, Catherine M. *365 Women's Reflections on Men.* Holbrook, Mass.: Adams Media, 1997.

Eisen, Armand. *Believing in Ourselves.* Kansas City, Mo.: Andrews McMeel, 1997.

———. *Witty Women: Wise, Wicked, and Wonderful Words.* Kansas City, Mo: Andrews McMeel, 1994.

Exley, Helen. *The Best of Women's Quotations.* New York: Exley Publications, 1993.

Johnson, Diane J. *Proud Sisters: The Wisdom and Wit of African-American Women.* White Plains, N.Y.: Peter Pauper Press, 1995.

King, Anita. *Contemporary Quotations in Black.* Westport, Conn.: Greenwood Press, 1997.

Lansky, Bruce. *Age Happens*. New York: Meadow-brook Press, 1996.

Maggio, Rosalie. *The New Beacon Book of Quotations by Women*. Boston: Beacon Press, 1996.

Malloy, Merrit. *Irish-American Funny Quotes*. New York: Sterling Publishing, 1994.

Metcalf, Fred. *The Penguin Dictionary of Modern Humorous Quotations*. New York: Penguin Books, 1986.

Porter, Dahlia, and Gabriel Cervantes. *365 Reflections on Fathers*. Holbrook, Mass.: Adams Media, 1998.

Princeton Language Institute. *Twenty-first Century Dictionary of Quotations*. New York: Dell Publishing, 1993.

Quinn, Tracy. *Quotable Women of the Twentieth Century*. New York: William Morrow, 1999.

Reagan, Michael, and Bob Phillips. *The All-American Quote Book*. Eugene, Oreg.: Harvest House, 1995.

Reed, Maxine. *And Baby Makes Three: Wise and Witty Observations on the Joys of Parenthood*. Chicago: Contemporary Books, 1995.

Silverman, Stephen M. *Funny Ladies: The Women Who Make Us Laugh*. New York: Harry N. Abrams, 1999.

Stibbs, Anne. *A Woman's Place: Quotations About Women*. New York: Avon Books, 1992.

The Wit and Wisdom of Women. Philadelphia: Running Press, 1993.

Wylie, Betty Jane. *Men! Quotations About Men, by Women*. Toronto: Key Porter Books, 1993.